INDIA IN TRANSITION

D1830343

Owing to the antiquity and rarity of this book, certain pages are regrettably absent, and readability is compromised due to the blurring of the original text. If you possess any insights regarding the availability of these missing sections, kindly inform us. Your assistance is crucial in ensuring the completion of this significant work for the benefit of future generations.

INDIA IN TRANSITION

A STUDY IN POLITICAL EVOLUTION

AGA SULTAN MAHOMED SHAH AGA KHAN

GYAN

Published by

Gyan Publishing House
5, Ansari Road
Daryaganj, New Delhi-110002
Phone: 011-47034999, 9811692060
E-mail: books@gyanbooks.com

Distribution Network
gyanbooks.com
India, USA, Canada, UK, Australia

© Publisher
All rights reserved. No part of this work may be reproduced, stored, adapted, or transmitted in any form or by any means, electronic, mechanical, photocopying, micro-filming, recording or otherwise, or translated in any language, without the prior written permission of the copyright owner and the publisher.

ISBN: 978-93-7133-331-3 (PB)
First Published, 1918

2nd Impression 2025

Printed at: Gyan Press, Delhi.

The book is sold subject to the condition that it shall not, by way of trade or otherwise, be lent, resold, hired out, or otherwise circulated without the prior publisher's written consent.

INDIA IN TRANSITION
Author Aga Sultan Mahomed Shah Aga Khan

INDIA IN TRANSITION

INDIA IN TRANSITION

A STUDY IN POLITICAL EVOLUTION

BY HIS HIGHNESS THE AGA KHAN

TO

MY MOTHER

FOREWORD

MR. MONTAGU'S historic announcement last August that he was to proceed to India to discuss the extent and form of the "substantial steps" to be taken in the direction of self-governing institutions, and to receive with Lord Chelmsford the suggestions of representative bodies and others, confirmed me in the intention I had formed on finding I was debarred on medical grounds from Army service in the Allied cause to return to India last winter. I cherished the hope that I might be of some small service to my country in helping to shape some of the representations which might be made, and in contributing to the success of so momentous a mission by a British statesman whose zeal and devotion in promoting the welfare of India had greatly impressed the Indian people during the time of his Under-Secretaryship at the India Office.

My plans and hopes were thwarted, however, by a painful and tedious malady requiring surgical treatment in Europe, and fully six months of rest and retirement in a prescribed climate. The eminent specialists consulted were peremptory in refusing my appeal to be permitted to carry out my plans. They were confident that within two or three weeks of my landing in Bombay I should be laid aside by severe illness, making it quite impossible for me to render the public service I had in view. Their assurances that acceptance of their advice and the regimen prescribed would most probably restore me to vigorous health are being confirmed as time goes on.

The bitterness of my disappointment was considerably mitigated when, acting on the suggestion of valued friends, I obtained the assent of the specialists to my spending two or three hours daily during my enforced retirement and rest in consecutive literary work, for the purpose of presenting a detailed exposition of my views on Indian reconstruction. I had been approached frequently in the past dozen years or so by publishing houses with requests to write a book on current topics. Though the idea was not without attraction, I did not consider that the time was ripe to bring it to fruition; and I continued to limit my public utterances to speeches in India and in England, and to occasional review and newspaper articles. I now felt it a duty, as well as a privilege, to give a detailed exposition of my thoughts on India, and my hopes and aspirations for the future, as a contribution to the many-sided problem Mr. Montagu has been investigating.

The reader will pardon, I trust, these personal details since they are required for an understanding of the conditions in which my views have been formulated and presented. They may be pleaded in mitigation of shortcomings in execution, of which I am only too conscious. In my retirement the verification of references has not been easy, nor have I had the opportunities of consultation on questions of fact or policy which might otherwise have been available. The revision of proofs, in the later stages, I have been compelled to leave to others, in order to obviate any greater delay than present difficulties of book production in England imposes.

My limitations, however, have not been without their compensations. Enforced exclusion from the arena of day by day discussion in India, however disappointing, may have contributed at least to the dispassionateness with which I have sought to temper the ardour of my Indian patriotism and my belief in the inherent possibilities of my countrymen under the more favourable political conditions I advocate. Though outside the current, I have been able to watch its course with the help of many kind correspondents and occasional visitors, and by careful study of the organs of opinion in India.

Moreover, writing and thinking almost within hearing of the thunder of battle in Europe, I have been in a better position to apply to the Indian problem the widened outlook derived from a close and frequent contact with political systems and affairs outside, as well as within, my own country. Further, thrown so fully on my own resources, I can at least claim that the work, whatever its demerits, is an original and strictly personal contribution to the Indian problem. Many of the opinions I express will not be new to leaders of political and social thought in many lands with whom for years past I have discussed the future of India. Such views can also be traced in my occasional writings, though they have undergone development in the last four fateful years. We none of us stand where we did before the events of July and August, 1914, brought us to the watershed of contemporary history. The war has enormously changed the political and social outlook throughout the world in the direction of strengthening those forces of democracy and national self-determination, of liberty and progress, for which the Allies have made so many sacrifices.

One further word of explanation is desirable. I have studiously avoided any attempt to penetrate the plans which may have been formulated by the Secretary of State and the Viceroy as a result of their consultations, and which have still to be disclosed at the time I write. I make no claim to any inspiration in the guise of "intelligent anticipation." The proposals of His Majesty's Government are to be issued for public discussion, and will be embodied in a Bill to be submitted to Parliament in due course. I cherish the hope that this contribution to the subject may be of some service in helping to mould the moderate yet earnestly progressive ideas, both in Great Britain and India, on which, when all is said, the satisfactory and continuous solution of the complex Indian problem depends.

AGA KHAN.

18 *May*, 1918.

CONTENTS

CONTENTS

INDIA IN TRANSITION

CHAPTER I

SOCIAL ORGANISATION

FOR profitable study of the problems of a country, not only has the political evolution of its inhabitants to be considered, but also the history of their social customs, their economic and legal institutions and ideas, and the spiritual influences that have gone to make them what they are. In the case of India the issues are of unique complexity.

Laying aside all prejudices and looking upon the progress of mankind from the wild and primitive state whence civilisation has been evolved, we find that the early history of development takes two main divisions. The first is represented by the various societies that have advanced from disorganised and, at most, tribal institutions, till they have reached the forms of civilised life represented by laws, civic institutions, systematised religion, and those comforts and luxuries and dreams of beauty to which, in their highest forms, we give the name of Arts. The second stage is the life of the savage tribes as they exist to-day in North America, in the Arctic and Sub-Arctic regions, in the Pacific, in Africa and, in a small way, in India and on her far-stretched frontiers.

For the purposes of present study, we need not take the earlier stages into consideration, and can confine ourselves to the developed societies. But here new and clearly-marked divisions arise. Disregarding Aztec civilisation, since it was destroyed by the Conquistadores, and has left only indirect influences in Mexico and parts of Central and South America, the world of to-day contains four principal and clearly-defined forms of civilisation. These we will take *seriatim.*

To the first we give the name " Western." It is the body of institutions, customs, etc., common alike to Germany and England, to Chile and Russia in Europe, to Bulgaria and Australia, to Scandinavia and to the Latin States of South America. The moulding influences have been wide and varied: Greek and Roman civilisation, and the many religions that arose in the first century of the Christian era in the Eastern and the Western provinces of the Roman Empire; Christianity and its chequered history; then the Reformation and the counter-Reformation, the hundred and one spiritual movements which, like ripples on a lake, rose and fell in the various churches of the West. Who that has come from another civilisation can fail to see everywhere in the far-reaching areas which I have indicated the influences of Saint Theresa and Saint Francis of Assisi, of Luther and Calvin, of Seneca and Plato, of Lucretius and Homer, of Giordano Bruno and Newton, of Goethe and Darwin ?

But this civilisation contains many other important elements. It is the one most permeated by the influences of those processes of watching and interpreting natural phenomena, to which we give the name of Science. Indeed, the modern inductive method is almost a monopoly of this division of our culture. It has so constantly wrested from Nature her secrets for material purposes, that one can almost say it stands alone in knowing how to bring into the service of mankind the more recondite forces of the inanimate world. Further, its artistic and æsthetic standards and judgments are similarly peculiar to itself. In poetry, in architecture, in painting and sculpture, its achievements are so different from those of the contemporary cultures, yet with such a family resemblance, that anyone belonging to the latter realises, at the very first contact, that here is a great and homogeneous development of the human spirit.

In music Western culture is far in advance of its contemporaries. Its social customs have a certain uniformity that cannot be mistaken for those of the latter. For instance, monogamy and its apparently inevitable drawback, the social evil of the recognised existence of the fallen sisterhood, are everywhere in evidence. In economics, the vast numbers engaged in production largely for the benefit of absent and anonymous owners, to whom we give the name of joint stock companies, differentiate this Western organisation from all others. There is throughout the lands of its supremacy a certain general uniformity of life and ideas and institutions, as of one great family. However distinct its branches may be, there is in all a resemblance that leaves no doubt of the essential unity. Santiago de Chile and Moscow,

Sofia and New York, Berlin and Melbourne, have a basic similarity that is apparent immediately we try to compare these or any other Western cities with, say, Tokio or Teheran.

Though predominant, this Western civilisation is not without rivals. There are three others still in the world, each counting its children and devotees by the hundred millions. First of these, in our survey, we take the culture of the Far East. This name is no less inadequate than the term "Western" in the first of these divisions, but is probably the most general and characteristic word which we can use. Here, too, there are vast differences between the customs and psychology of, say, the Japanese and the Tibetans, or of the Manchus and the Burmans; but there is also a distinct general similarity of fundamental ideas, habits, and outlook upon life, from Tibet to Japan, from the Amur River to the Irrawaddy. The thoughtful visitor from Europe or America is at once struck by a certain correspondence that permeates these vast territories and their myriad inhabitants. No doubt, between the Japanese and the Burmans the gulf is so great that the influence of Buddhism may almost be called the only connecting link; but when we compare either race or the Chinese, with, say, the South Americans or the people of Morocco, we are impressed by a certain harmony of the Far Eastern cultures. It must not be concluded that there is any racial unity. The Japanese and the Chinese probably come from different original stocks, and again the Tibetans and the Burmans are probably different in origin from the Chinese. But, as in the West the many races of Europe and America have been drawn together by spiritual ideals and social influences; so, in the Far East, similar potencies have worked for a unity of civilisation which is to-day apparent everywhere, from the Pacific to the Bay of Bengal, and from the Northern slopes of the Himalayas to Siberia.

The third civilisation, for want of a better term, we may call Brahmanical. It is found everywhere in India amongst the millions who come from the originally fair foreign stocks. It has permeated myriads of the descendants of the dark aboriginals of the country, raising them into a far higher stage of culture than that of the Bhils and other tribes who still remain in a primitive state. The Brahmanical characteristics are well known to all who have been to India or studied its history and literature. Unlike the other living civilisations, its influence, while absolute over some 230,000,000 human beings, is mainly confined to one political entity; though it is not unknown outside the limits of India. In Malaysia and in the Pacific Archipelago, Brahmanical influences have been great in the past and are evident to-day. If ever a truly Irredentist movement were started in India it would be sure to draw the Brahmanical peoples of that country towards the millions of the islands and peninsulas of Java and Sumatra, the Straits Settlements and Borneo. We must always remember that the Brahmans are only a small minority of the people of these lands; but the stamp of Brahmanical civilisation, with the dominance of the priestly caste, has been once and for all impressed on many races who have nothing else in common with the Aryan invaders.

The fourth main civilisation we call Islamic, or Mahomedan, after the great Founder whose personality still dominates all his spiritual children. It is apparent from the Atlantic to Java, and from the Balkans to the Himalayas. Within it are very distinct and different races, such as the white Berbers of Morocco and Algeria, the Arnauts of Albania (perhaps the purest European race) and the many converted Serbs of Bosnia and Macedonia. Then there are the hundreds of millions of every colour and race in Africa, Arabia, Persia, Central Asia, India, China, and the Malay Archipelago. But wherever Islam exists there is the manifest influence of its Founder, that permeates all classes and races. Arabian and Persian culture, too, in architecture, in arts, and in literature is evident wherever Islam is found. You cannot visit a Moslem city without immediately being struck by the minaret of the mosque, which is everywhere the first sign of Islam, turned upwards towards the Great Beyond. The strong mystic influence that permeates Moslem nations cannot be mistaken for any other spiritual force than that of the Koran. There is the less agreeable phase, too, of a certain other-worldliness and coldly calculating devotion which is perhaps inevitable where millions devoutly believe that this world is nothing but a bridge towards Eternity.

It has not been my purpose to give more than the most general description of these four great currents of progress, in order to show that they are the principal lines on which the human spirit has developed. The fact has an intimate bearing on the issues to be discussed in this book, for in India, and in India alone of all the great countries of the world, these four civilisations are each largely and powerfully represented.

This co-existence of the four main surviving streams of human culture is the dominant fact of Indian life. Side by side with them are the relatively tiny rills of semi-savage races and tribes, scarcely more advanced than any that Africa can show, scattered chiefly in the hills and forests of the South, the central areas, the East and the North-East, and in the Andaman Islands. At the last census the Animistic tribes numbered some 10,300,000 persons.

The main streams have many tributaries, from greater or lesser differences of race and history, of religion and tradition. Special note must be taken of Jewry, that influential and distinctive connecting link between Western and Islamic civilisations. Both Mussulman and Christian are deeply indebted for the foundations of their faiths to its traditional and exalted theology, and while, like Islam, it is Semitic in origin, it is largely Western in outlook and distribution. In India there are anciently settled Jewish colonies on the Bombay and Malabar coasts. But, keeping to our main classification of human cultures, we must see how each of the four reached India, and appraise their relative importance in her life and history.

The oldest and the most powerful of them is the Brahmanical culture. It is the original foundation of Indian society, and to this day it retains sway over at least two-thirds of the population.

Next comes the Islamic, alike in point of age and numerical importance. It entered India through Sind as early as the end of the seventh century, and thereafter greatly increased. To this advance the successive invasions from the North-West, the Arabian influences carried across the Indian Ocean to Western India, and missionary effort, such as was carried on in Bengal in the eighteenth century, all contributed. Islam has become by now a truly national institution in India, and its adherents form nearly a fifth of the population.

Third in date, but politically the most important to-day, stands Western civilisation. It reached India from the thirteenth century onwards, first through the medium of Venetian, Portuguese, Spanish, Dutch, French, and British traders, physicians, and adventurers. Later came powerful commercial corporations belonging to some of these nationalities, and the military and political organisations established by the Portuguese, the Dutch, the French, and the British at coast factories. The Indian foreign history of the seventeenth and eighteenth centuries is, to a great extent, that of the contests for supremacy of these traders from the West and of the varying co-operation which each competing European nation obtained in India in its own support. However, the Dutch disappeared entirely from the peninsula, though they still have the most splendid of existing colonial empires, next to that of England, in the rich islands of the Pacific. The Portuguese and the French retain small footholds on the West and East coasts respectively, and thus contribute slightly to the representation of Western civilisation in India. But it is the British alone who have carried their power and influence throughout the length and breadth of India and well beyond her borders ; who have not only secured political supremacy, but have drawn many sections of

Indian society under the influence of Western civilisation. They have been the chief agents in essential general forms of that culture, such as the watching and interpretation of Nature around us, to which we give the name of Science; the use of mechanical forces in industry and transport, and the voluntary union of capital, now being accepted and applied by every class in India. Further, Britain, Portugal, and France, with American and other foreign assistance in modern times, have won over small, yet powerful and growing sections of society to Christianity, and have thus sown the seeds of dominant Western influence. Yet again, in the domiciled European and Anglo-Indian communities Western civilisation has direct and permanent representatives.

Last in order as an integral part of Indian life came Far Eastern influences. From the beginning of the nineteenth century onwards, inevitable causes, but whose action was precipitated by the fact of British dominion over India, brought British and Indian forces, commercial, political, and military, into Burma, and fifteen years before the century closed the entire province, with its essentially Far Eastern social organisation, had become an integral part of India united to the other and fundamentally different societies of that great land by political, commercial, and other bonds. Severance of the political tie has sometimes been suggested, but becomes more and more improbable. Thus, India has not only grown in power and population, but has absorbed into her system the weaker countries beyond.

This process has not been confined to the East and the absorption of Burma. North-westwards,

Baluchistan, an essentially Islamic country, has been drawn by forces beyond human control into the orbit of India; the Durand line marks a definite extension of the "political" boundary in the Pathan country; while across the Arabian Sea Aden and the small protected principalities of the Gulf littoral have been for many years within the territories under Indian Government control. These essentially Mahomedan and foreign lands have been, in the widest sense of the word, Indian, and the political outlook of the inhabitants of Aden[1] or Lahej has not been, in essentials, different from that of the people of Karachi or Janjira.

It must not be concluded that this process of extension has reached its ultimate stage. On the contrary, probably artificial causes have prevented the great united Empire which England has raised in India from making its influence felt on all the surrounding countries to the limits of her natural expanding power. Throughout the nineteenth century, when India exercised far less direct or indirect influence on British policy than she has done in the present decade, issues of European diplomacy made the independence of Persia and the continued supremacy of Turkey in Mesopotamia and Eastern Arabia the foundation of British policy in the Gulf. This necessarily led to the limitation of Indian expansion alike in trade and in political influence, over the thinly-populated lands lying to the west of India. Can anyone deny that, if the Mogul Empire had not been dissolved, or if

[1] Lord Curzon stated in the House of Lords on December 4, 1917, that though for war purposes, the political charge of Aden is now under the Home Government, the question of an absolute transfer from the Indian Government could not be forcibly determined until after the conclusion of peace.

it had been succeeded by a powerful and united Hindu Empire over the whole of India, the lands of the Persian Gulf littoral would long ago have been brought under Indian dominance? Nor can the process of Indian expansion westwards be stopped by any series of treaties or political conditions. Whatever else happens, and whatever the flag that may hereafter float over Basra and Bagdad, over Bushire and Muscat, Indian civilisation, commerce, and emigration must become an increasing power in Mesopotamia, Persia, and Arabia. This process will add greatly to Mahomedan influence in India itself, while, on the other hand, by taking Hindu influences into lands hitherto regarded as the preserves of Islam, it must inevitably lead to a better understanding between the Brahmanical and the Islamic peoples of the peninsula.

Nor are Indian expansion and influence found in Asia alone. Before the advent of British rule Indian maritime relations and trade had been established on the shores of East Africa. An Indian business colony, much on the lines of the Greek trading communities of Southern France and Italy, grew up and was firmly planted by the end of the eighteenth century. Throughout the nineteenth century, its members were the standard-bearers of civilisation on the coast and in the then extended dominions of the Sultan of Zanzibar. When those vast lands were divided between England, Germany, and Italy in the last quarter of the cycle the Indian settlers became, through natural and inevitable causes, the pillars of the civilised European governments and the go-betweens in commerce and administration. In

British East Africa the railways have been laid by Indian labour, and technical and industrial work which is far beyond the capacity of the African tribes and yet below the standard of imported European efficiency, has been carried on by Indians. This is to a lesser extent true of the territory hitherto known as German East Africa.

The expansion I have described has not been limited to pacific penetration or to the effects of the present war. Northwards, by blunders, by mistakes, by want of policy if you will, but still inevitably, as if it were merely a natural force, pushing on the currents of Indian life to Afghanistan and Tibet, these countries also have been drawn into the orbit of India.

Sooner or later, whatever the preferences of the peoples of those closed lands may be, and whatever the policy of their rulers, yet so strong are the forces of civilisation that these countries will not be able to maintain their political and economic isolation. They will need the goods of Europe and the Far East, more of the products of India and her manufactures of a more elaborate kind than hitherto. To provide exchange of commodities development of the undoubted mineral wealth of these countries will be necessary. There will also be a far larger export of fruits and preserves that cannot be easily grown in India proper and the culture of which has been for many centuries a regular, though limited, occupation in Afghanistan and parts of Tibet. For geographical and other reasons therefore these States must draw on Indian help and assistance for their instruction and efficiency. European civilisation will thus reach them second-hand; but so great is the poverty of these secluded mountainous regions that they can only obtain supplies from a cheap country like India instead of from Europe. It may be urged that both Afghanistan and Tibet will turn to some stable element that possibly may be evolved from present chaos in Russian lands; but a study of geographical facts will convince any open-minded observer that through Central Asia, with its sparse population, dismembered Russia with a rigorous winter climate and hemmed in from the sea, cannot be the natural helper or the commercial mainstay of these countries.

Thus, looking forward a few years, at most a decade or two, we may anticipate an economic, commercial, and intellectual India not bounded by the vast triangle of the Himalayas on the north and the Indian Ocean and Bay of Bengal on either side down to Adam's Bridge, but consisting of a vast agglomeration of states, principalities and countries in Asia extending from Aden to Mesopotamia, from the two shores of the Gulf to India proper, from India proper across Burma and including the Malay Peninsula; and then from Ceylon to the States of Bokhara, and from Tibet to Singapore. The aggregation might well be called the "South Asiatic Federation," of which India would be the pivot and centre.

Thus the Indian problem, taken in its widest connotations, directly affects nearly 400,000,000 human beings, made up of races manifold, so different as Arabs and Burmans, Tibetans and Singalese, Afghans and Bengalees, Mahrattas and Malays. As already noted, while all the four great existing civilisations are here strongly represented, side by side with them are handfuls of semi-savage men, who have not even taken the first steps towards an elementary intellectual development. Then there are the hundred and one principalities and provinces, minor races and sects, with their local histories, their faded glories and their future hopes. Everywhere, whether directly or indirectly, it is Britain that stands for law and order, for the cement between the ancient cultures of the East and those both ancient and modern of the West; Britain who, in spite of European rivalries, is still for these hundreds of millions of people the only white and Western Power.

Such is the tremendous problem before us. The future of the Iberian Republics of the New World, the existence or disruption of China, the continuation of rivalry or the dawn of reconciliation and union in Europe—these are the only three other great world issues that can be compared in importance to that which, with diffidence and an appeal for the forbearance and patience of my readers, I discuss in the ensuing chapters.

CHAPTER II

THE REASONS FOR REFORM

SOON after undertaking the preparation of this book I was set thinking by a conversation with one of the most distinguished of present-day British publicists, the greatest living authority on Russia and Central and Eastern Europe. His keen intimacy with world politics embraces mankind from China to Peru, but alas! in the course of his long and busy life he has never had occasion to visit India or specially study her affairs. He asked me why India required any marked change of system. Taking into consideration the divisions of the people, the illiteracy of the masses, the rivalries of religions and races, he asked why, confronted by all this clash and backwardness, England could not go on more or less as she had done throughout the nineteenth century, and rule her vast Asiatic dominions with undivided but conscientiously exercised authority.

My friend maintained that divisions being deep and real and political harmony being confined to a small minority of the upper and educated classes, there will be no real need for a change of policy until such time as the masses insist on their rights and take a share in the responsibilities of government. His purpose was, I think, to draw from me a reasoned statement of the case for reform.

Coming from the incisive critic alike of the reign and policy of Alexander III and of the ultra-democratic Bolshevists of the hour this view seemed to me singularly unconvincing. If there is one thing which modern history proves, it is this: that unless the government and the governing classes take up the task of raising the masses of the people gradually, but surely, thus founding the fabric of the commonwealth on the widest and deepest basis possible, namely, the whole population, the State renders itself liable to years and years of anarchy and disaster, and perhaps to dissolution.

Look at the Russian portent. Had Alexander II lived a few years longer, had the policy of Loris Milikoff been carried out in 1881, had the last twenty years of the nineteenth century been occupied with construction and education, with uniting the people and the government, and with the evolution of self-government in the various provinces, how different and how happy and healthy Russian history would have been! Taking another instance, the disastrous reign of Abdul Hamid in Turkey might have been one of revivifying forces, had that astute but misguided sovereign devoted the same period to the work of gradual association of the people with the government on the one hand, and to social and cultural development of the masses on the other. In China, had the late Empress-Dowager initiated her death-bed scheme of gradual reform twenty-five years sooner, would that countless and intelligent nation have been to-day a danger to herself and her neighbours, and a real source of weakness to humanity at large?

Conversely there are examples of countries where

a wise and patriotic aristocracy, in association with an intelligent monarchy belonging to the soil, has worked wonders and has so interwoven the interests of every class that even the Socialists are to-day the pillars of the State. Japan is a case in point, and Prussia, whatever its severity and remorselessness towards outside peoples, provides an instance of successful consolidation of all classes through gradual steps of greater association of the people with the government. England herself supplies the outstanding clear-cut example of this healthy development, though she differs from the two other instances quoted by her work having been almost unconscious. Instead of taking place in two centuries, as in Prussia, and in two generations, as in Japan, it has gone on from the dawn of English history.

If the British, on whom historical causes have thrown the ultimate responsibility for the future of India and of surrounding states and nations, were to fail in this their greatest task, Southern Asia would become the theatre of one of the heaviest disasters humanity has faced. Sooner or later, an ignorant and innumerable proletariat, extending over nearly the whole length of Asia from the Red Sea to the Pacific, divided by religion and race and language, would be faced with the problem of self-government and self-development. The course of Russian history in our times provides a tragic warning to those who are responsible for the future of India of the dangers of leaving the apparently well alone, and of not working for the development of the masses in rights and duties alike and in responsibility towards society. It has been well said that the

British tenure in India must be one of continuous amelioration.

But apart from these lessons of modern history we have to recognise the existence of internal forces in India proper and in the neighbouring states and principalities that render a policy of standing still or of merely nominal concession a practical impossibility since it would work disaster, in the long run, alike for Britain and for India. These forces may not individually be powerful enough to compel renunciation of existing forms of government; but, taken together and in connection with other world forces which react even in remote portions of Southern Asia, they are so enormous in their effect that a radical change of outlook is necessary. A brief examination of some of the more important of them is desirable.

In the forefront we must place the fact that until the summer of 1914 there was a white and European solidarity *vis-à-vis* Asia and Africa which, though officially unrecognized, was yet the foundation of European policy in the widest sense of the term. A small but suggestive point of nomenclature illustrates my meaning. The British governing classes and the white mercantile community were referred to throughout India as "Europeans," and the general line of differentiation as between the governors and the governed was shown by the terms "European" and "Native," or latterly the more acceptable cognomen "Indian." There were many other signs of the concert of Europe at work, though of course officially unrecognised. The German, French or Italian trader or missionary had social union with the British rulers and business men, carrying inherent privileges that made them members of the same governing European family. But the Great War has broken up that solidarity. The German and Austrian missionary and trader has been interned in India or repatriated, and all and sundry have watched the humiliation of these fallen members of the white race. The most remote villagers have heard of the sepoys who have fought hand to hand with the fairest inhabitants of Europe. The long-maintained racial line of demarcation has been largely replaced by that of allegiance to Sovereign and flag.

For the full establishment of this sound guiding principle the claims of merit and fidelity must become predominant. By universal testimony this war has shown that the loyalty of the people of India to Emperor and Empire is second to none. In no other belligerent country, not even in Great Britain or Germany, have the forces of sedition and anarchy been so minute in proportion to the numbers of the law-abiding as in India. The small and insignificant factions which sought to create difficulties at a time of Imperial stress were but as a drop in the ocean, and all classes came forward to help England in her hour of trial. True the numbers of recruits, though vastly in excess of normal requirements, were small compared to the teeming population. But, as will be seen when we discuss the military needs of India, this was due to obvious historical, sociological, and political causes, not to any want of loyalty. Wherever and whenever any help could be given by the people of India, it was heartily bestowed. Can the annals of any other country ruled by an essentially foreign governing class responsible to an external Power, show the people coming forward and making equal sacrifices from patriotic motives?

The explanation of this now historic fact, so puzzling and disappointing to Teutonic enemies of England, is simple. Though to foreigners and onlookers India may be a conquered country, yet British rule was extended (with Indian help) so insidiously and so gradually, it has lasted so long and the work of conquest and administration has from the first been carried on by British heads and Indian hands to such an extent, that the average Indian does not look upon himself as belonging to a conquered people, or on his country as dominated by foreigners. He has awakened to the reality only when he has tried to visit the British self-governing Dominions, which have now agreed to a more liberal-minded policy. This altogether healthy Indian sentiment cannot last unless changes are introduced in the administration so as to give the people a fuller share and voice in the control of affairs in their own country. Many forces, internal and external, are working to awaken Indians in general, and the urban population in particular, to the reasonableness of their claims to a share in their own government.

And if we turn to neighbouring countries within the orbit of India we find that some have enjoyed to the present time forms of self-government, and others look upon themselves as conquering and independent races. Take the case of Mesopotamia. However bad Turkish rule there may have been, yet, even under Abdul Hamid's absolutist government, there was nominal equality of rights between Turk and Arab. Under the Young Turks, however insubstantial constitutional government may have been, the people of Baghdad and of Basra had the same rights of representation in the Chamber of Deputies as the people of Ismid or Adrianople, though in practice they were reduced to nothing of substantial value.

Yet if Mesopotamia is to become a British or a semi-British province, it is impossible to establish a purely bureaucratic administration among a people who have had at least nominal equality of opportunity with the Turkish rulers. Can it be seriously maintained that Britain can establish a government based in some degree on co-operation of the rulers and the ruled in Mesopotamia, and at the same time continue in India an administration in no sense responsible to the people? Though illiteracy is, alas! still general, though divisions, especially amongst the untaught masses, are deep, there is a general consensus of opinion amongst the upper and middle classes that the establishment of an administrative system more or less responsible to the people, and drawing its forces from their confidence and co-operation, cannot be long delayed.

We all know that the vast Indian majority consists of illiterate peasants and field labourers in the rural districts, but it must not be forgotten that the urban dwellers and the literate classes, though forming but a small proportion of the aggregate total, are still numerous enough to be equal to the population of a secondary European state. In 1911 the urban ratio was 9·5 per cent, and the census recorded more than 18½ million literates. Each year the schools and colleges and factories draw more and more from the great reservoir of the country districts to the towns and cities. No one familiar with modern India will deny that everywhere in the towns and in almost every class, there is a growing desire for a form of government that will allow the Indian to carry his head high as a citizen of a free Empire, and at the same time will provide the means for raising the lower classes of the rural population to a fuller standard of citizenship and life.

Again, a fundamental change has come over the Indian outlook on public affairs. I have often been told by English civilians that the Musulmans need another Sir Syed Ahmed, and that it is a pity that his political policy has disappeared. My answer has always been that Lord Beaconsfield and his Mahomedan policy are as dead as cold mutton. I am not sure if the gentlemen who started the conversation on these lines always realised what this answer conveyed. But here it is necessary to put on record the changed perspective within the last generation.

Twenty-five years ago the average Indian Moslem looked upon himself as a member of a universal religious brotherhood, sojourning in a land in which a neutral Government, with a neutral outlook, kept law and order and justice. His political and communal pride was satisfied by the fact that his co-religionists in Turkey, Persia, Morocco, and (nominally at least) in Egypt enjoyed independence and national sovereignty. While his allegiance was to Queen Victoria, his political self-respect was satisfied by the existence of the Sultans at Constantinople and Fez, and of the Shah and Khedive at Teheran and Cairo. The fact that the British Government was the mainstay and support in the diplomatic arena of the independent Mahomedan States was naturally a source of continued gratification to him. Far be it from me to suggest that all this was actually and consciously thought, and deductions made therefrom. But it is the semi-conscious and the sub-conscious that give atmosphere to national even more than to individual life. It was sub-conscious hostility towards Western Europe that drove Germany into war, and it was sub-conscious sentiment that early in the present century drew the peoples of England and France together, long before they were compelled to draw the sword for the defence of the liberty and civilisation of mankind.

Within this generation, the whole Mahomedan world-outlook has changed. Forces beyond Moslem control led to the disappearance of Mahomedan rule and independence in North Africa. Persia gradually drifted into being merely a name for spheres of influence between Britain and Russia. Turkey herself, the last of the independent Mahomedan dominions, was drawn into the Teutonic orbit, first through economic and semi-political causes, and finally by her participation in the Great War on the German side. I do not suggest that the destruction of the independence of these last Moslem States was conscious and deliberate; but so strong are the world forces of this generation that states and societies which have stood still for centuries have now been overthrown by the strong currents of European and American activity. The net result is that the Indian Mahomedan, instead of holding but the outposts of Islam in the East, sees around him nothing but Moslem societies in a far greater state of decay than his own. The banner of the Prophet is no longer in strong hands in North Africa or Persia, and Turkey has become the political enemy of England and a satrapy of Germany. Under these circumstances, he necessarily looks upon India more and more as the hope of his political freedom and as the centre that may still raise the other Mahomedan countries to a higher standard of civilisation.

Another point to be remembered is that while, under the old conditions, the Mahomedans were doomed to be nothing but a one-fifth minority in an overwhelmingly Brahmanical India, to-day, as the forces of disruption gain strength in Western Asia, it is not improbable that the South Asiatic Federation of to-morrow, of which India must be the centre and the pivot, will contain not only the 66½ millions of Indian Moslems, but the thirty or forty millions more Musulmans inhabiting South Persia, Mesopotamia, Arabia, and Afghanistan. If we turn from numbers to surface of territory, the Islamic provinces of South Asia will be almost as great in extent as the India of yesterday. Hence there is little danger of the Mahomedans of India being nothing but a small minority in the coming federation. No doubt these considerations, again, are sub-conscious and semi-conscious; but they are potent. The Indian Moslem of to-day is no more haunted by the fear of being a powerless minority; nor has he constantly to look for his sentimental satisfaction to the Islamic States outside India.

Turning our gaze from the Moslems to the vast Hindu population, we find among its educated members the feeling that the great conflict announced as a war for liberty and freedom, for the protection of self-development in small countries, such as Belgium and Serbia, carries for the Allies the implication that political freedom is the heritage of every nation, great or small. The principles that render the Allied cause just in Europe are of universal application, *mutatis mutandis,* and lead to the deduction that India, too, must be set on the path of self-government. At this moment India and Egypt are almost the only two stable and advanced great countries where the administration is not in any appreciable degree responsible to the people, and where the foundation of State polity is the theory that the government is superior to the governed. Some fifteen years ago, when, for instance, Lord Curzon and Lord Cromer ruled in India and in Egypt, Russia, Turkey, Persia, and China were all ruled on this principle. But recent transformations in those lands leave the position of India unique. China and the Russias are republics, with nominally the most democratic forms of government, and Persia and Turkey both claim to be considered constitutional monarchies. Thus, in India alone we have a Government that is not only in practice free from internal parliamentary control, but is actually based on the principle that final decisions are in the hands of an administration not responsible to the people, although some opportunities for criticism are given in the Viceregal and provincial legislatures. The contradictory position of the Government leads to its being open to attack from all quarters, and yet to its being considered anomalous that Indians, alone of the great Eastern peoples, should have no control over their administration. These causes, and many others, have led to general expectation and desire throughout the length and breadth of India that, when the cause of liberty as represented by the Allied armies has led humanity through victory to peace, the structure of Indian administration also may be brought into line with the spirit of the times and a reasonable share of control and supervision be given to the Indian public.

If we turn to the Native States and to the fully or semi-independent countries, such as Afghanistan and Nepal and the Arabian principalities, we find a general recognition on the part of the authorities that the time is coming for sharing their powers with the ruled. The best administered of the Native States and most of the princes desire to establish some form of legislative or other constitutional government. This would serve the two-fold purpose of giving their States the prestige and force of national institutions, and the ruling houses the claim of being united with the people by the ties of co-operation in the work of administration. In Afghanistan some attempt, howsoever nominal, has been made by the present King to lay the foundations of a representative institution. In fact everywhere in South Asia we find local forces striving, if sometimes unconsciously, after forms of administration more or less modern in character and leading to association and co-operation between the sovereign power and the nation. It follows that however excellent the present administration of India may be, however efficient and suited to the conditions of the recent past, it is not for the people of England to deny to their great Eastern Empire those forms of constitutionalism which were first developed in Britain and with the manifestations of which, whether in infancy or vigorous growth, England has always sympathised in the case of other countries on the European, American, and Asiatic continents.

Apart from the general considerations examined hitherto, there are administrative reasons which render imperative a change of system and policy. To begin with, no sounder political theory has been laid down than that maintained by the English economists, namely, good finance is the foundation of good government. It was bad finance that broke up the monarchy in France, and the most disastrous of present-day examples, Turkey and Russia, point to the same conclusion—that without sound finance ruin overtakes society. In India innumerable Viceroys, Secretaries of State and other competent observers have always held that good finance is fundamental to the moral authority of British rule. If this has been the case in the past, when the work of government was limited, how much more so to-day and to-morrow, when civilised societies expect from their governments the righting of social wrongs, thorough handling of the problems of sanitation and public instruction, and the establishment of a certain level of well-being as the inherent right of every citizen ?

Now, British rule in India has been criticised, and rightly criticised, for having allowed the twentieth century to dawn and grow without having grappled fully and successfully with the illiteracy general in India, and with the insanitary environment of the masses so bad that avoidable deaths are counted by the million every year, while the standard of the physique of the masses is deplorably low. The various modern departments of State that lead towards social betterment and social welfare in the West have still to be organised. The Indian public conscience unanimously demands that British rule should come into line with progressive modern ideas and tackle illiteracy and other social problems left far too long unsolved.

We shall be told, rightly, that at bottom, these are questions of bearable taxation. How are we to provide the means for meeting such crying needs of India? There are only two ways: either by co-operation between the Government and the governed and by discussion, proving to the representatives of the people the need, and thus making the Indian public itself the judge of the extent of the necessary sacrifice; or by mere fiat and mandate of the Supreme Government imposing taxation. Lord Cromer always held in conversations which I had with him that a government such as that of Britain in India and Egypt could not maintain itself except by light taxation, and Lord Morley's lately published "Recollections" show him to be of a like opinion. But Lord Cromer's own rule at Cairo laid itself open to the pointed criticism that while the Egyptian peasant grew rich he remained dirty and ignorant, superstitious and slovenly. Does not this go to prove that bureaucratic government, when well-intentioned and paternal, is conscious of some lack of moral right to call for those sacrifices from the people that will raise their condition in the cultural and sociological field *pari passu* with, or in advance of, their economic progress?

In India, however, it is far too late to adopt Lord Cromer's policy of light taxation in preference to modern advancement. The best rulers of Native

States have endeavoured in their relatively small way to solve the problems of illiteracy and social betterment. The leaders of India unanimously expect from their Government the steady provision of those agencies which in Europe and America have brought about the fusion of culture between the masses and the classes. It is for the Government to take steps necessary to find the means for carrying out this policy, and this can be done with the co-operation of the representatives of the people and by discussion that will prove to the rulers and the ruled that the resources to be tapped are those that can best bear the burden of greater taxation.

If we turn from the problem of finance to the only other equally important and equally essential principle of government, namely, that of defence, we are forced to the same conclusion: that the sharing of responsibility between the people of India and its government is now necessary. I earnestly cherish the hope of President Wilson that a society of nations may result from the tremendous cost and suffering of these years of conflict, and I am convinced that forms of arbitration and limitation of armaments, through international agencies of control, will arise after the war. Yet no one who looks at the problem of Asia to-day can doubt that India must be prepared and ready to defend herself. Whether Britain keeps Mesopotamia, or whether that rich but neglected land becomes an independent principality or republic under British suzerainty, or whether it goes back to some form of Turkish control, yet its economic relations with India must so grow as to give us in practice a trans-Gulf frontier to defend. The same is true of

Persia, and if we look Eastwards, with the growth of Japan and with the problem of our North-East frontier touching China, we cannot afford to neglect India's potentialities.

Now, a small and professional army, such as India had and has to-day, can never possess the reserves and the natural expanding power to meet modern war, with its terrible casualties, with its heavy technical services, with its lines of communication to be conserved and defended. While the Russias will not trouble us for generations, Germany, directly or indirectly, has become an Asiatic Power. Assuming that Turkey loses Mesopotamia and Syria, German military organisation will yet still be supreme on the other side of the Taurus Mountains and in the uplands of Asia Minor. Howsoever friendly modern Japan may be, and howsoever impotent modern China, yet India can never again be left to depend merely on Japanese goodwill and Chinese weakness for her security against attack from the East. Just as Australia, although she has the sea to protect her from sudden attack, has had to organise her defensive forces on modern lines by universal training, so the India of the next decade must develop her internal forces in such a way as to be able to meet any sudden emergency.

In India, with its 315,000,000 inhabitants, universal military service can be hardly feasible and probably will never be necessary; yet some form of fairly distributed national service falling on, say, 10 per cent of the inhabitants of each locality, to be selected by purely physical tests of healthiness and efficiency, can alone meet her problem of defence. No doubt the military training here referred to will not be the two or three years of the German and French Armies, but rather the six months of the Swiss forces. Such is, in fact, the proposal contained in a Territorial scheme submitted to the Indian Government in 1916. Still, this will be such a tax on the energy and life of the people that it is inconceivable that any country should willingly accept it without the imprimatur of her elected spokesmen; nor can such representation be merely nominal as at present. It must comprise men drawn directly from the masses and from every locality.

Thus, from the two essential points of view of finance and defence alike, we come to the conclusion that a higher standard of citizenship, with both greater sacrifices and greater responsibilities, must be imposed on the people if the great work of Britain is not to end in failure. The accomplishment of the task which destiny has placed before England cannot be complete unless India is raised, through social laws and institutions, to the standard of at least a backward European or Spanish-American country. The necessary corollary is that India must be so able to defend herself from foreign aggression as to make her independent of the mere goodwill or the accidental and temporary impotence of her neighbours. Yet neither of these two great conditions can be brought about without the co-operation, through representative institutions, of the people with the Government, and without a thorough change of system that unites the administration with the masses by constant discussion leading to unity of aim between the direct representatives of the people and the highest officers of the Crown.

Thus, from several principal points of view and apart from the many minor lines of argument that lead to the same conclusions, we see that the Government of India needs radical change; that the time has come when it should be no more a mere government of fiat, however excellent the fiat, but an essentially modern State based on the co-operation of every community and of the Government, by giving to the people themselves the right to direct policy. In succeeding chapters I hope to show that this metamorphosis will not only lead to the happiness and contentment of India, but to the strengthening of the British Empire as a whole and to drawing India nearer to England and the Dominions.

CHAPTER III

A FEDERAL BASIS

THE perusal of the last chapter might lead the man in the street to the facile conclusion that the grant of representative assemblies, such as European States possess, would meet the needs of India, and that a full plan of co-operation between rulers and the ruled could be easily brought about by an edict from the King-Emperor. No such short cut to constitutionalism will do in India. To begin with, parliamentary government so far has been markedly successful only in countries of relatively small area, however populous any such given area may be. England, France, Germany, Sweden, Italy—you find no country with a greater surface than two or three hundred thousand square miles. We can draw no conclusions from the constitutions of Canada, Australia, and some of the South American republics, because these States are still at the dawn of national life; their populations are but handfuls compared to what they must be when full development is reached. At present society is limited to certain large cities and emporiums of trade, and small, widely scattered rural communities. In the United States, on the other hand, the very name of the country shows that the Republic consists of independent parliamentary communities.

This view of a State, relatively small in area or population, as the best foundation of parliamentary government was held by Bismarck, as I learned from his son, Count Herbert, in Berlin, only two years after the death of the founder of United Germany. In the course of a long conversation about a federation that has been fraught with such momentous consequences to mankind, Herbert Bismarck told me that one of the features which led his father to expect a successful development was that the great majority of administrative affairs would remain in the hands of each of the individual States of the Bundesrat. The Reichstag would deal only with questions relating to the Army, Foreign, and Maritime affairs. Bismarck maintained to the end that organic parliamentary union, such as exists in France and in the United Kingdom, would break down in Germany since the empire, instead of being a compact geographical unit, was a long and scattered dominion. If this could be said of Germany, how much truer it is of far wider empires. And since Russia secured some parliamentary freedom, we have seen inevitable causes leading to her break-up into smaller state organisms. Though the present rush of disruptive forces may be the result of war, ignorance, and the long period of misgovernment, can anyone doubt that, at best, liberty and freedom in Russia would have led to her division into component states ?

If, on the other hand, it is maintained that modern science, through vast railways and still more through rapid aerial navigation, has reduced distances, and that probably before the next few years are over aerial travelling will further abridge them, this contention will not remove the condition that only the geographically small parliamentary unit can be free and great. For, as we see, while Science on the one side brings distant places nearer, on the other hand, by giving intensive culture to localities and by highly developing local economic interests, it undoes the results of its first and apparent action. In a large primitive area, while distances are énormous and means of communication few, yet unless great natural obstacles, such as mountains and seas, arise, there is a general similarity of interest and occupation that makes for homogeneity. On the other hand, the higher the development of modern civilisation on a continent, the more heterogeneous and individual its parts become. And if this be true of Europe, with its single type of culture, it is far more applicable to India, where all the four main civilisations of the world are found, and where the problem is still further complicated by relatively minor differences of race, religion, history, and development.

Even in a political entity so small in area as the United Kingdom, independently of the embittered controversies caused by Ireland's racial and religious differences, the legislative combination of England and Wales, Scotland and Ireland has presented serious practical drawbacks. The efficiency of the Mother of Parliaments is notoriously hampered by the excessive pressure of detailed work, and the impossibility of more than a few members possessing the requisite local knowledge in reference to private bills, and the other wants of varying districts. Suggestions for the setting up of local parliaments, not only for Ireland and Scotland, but for Wales and homogeneous portions of England, were being made with increasing acceptance before the energies of the

Empire had to be concentrated on the mighty task still in hand. France has had a centralised form of government for centuries and, except amongst some of the people of Brittany, and the Basque of the Pyrenees, is as united a nation as can be desired. Yet even in France there are thinkers, in the South at all events, who have yearnings for local parliaments. One of the most successfully governed countries of the world, Switzerland, where you find the ideal combination of liberty and order, is ruled by small, freely elected parliaments over cantons of such compact dimensions that each citizen is a real participant in the affairs of his province. This illustration is specially important because Switzerland, on a small scale, like India on a large one, consists of different nationalities grouped by political union.

Whatever may be said of the general merits of the Indian reform scheme outlined in the joint address of a number of prominent Indians and Europeans submitted to the Viceroy and the Secretary of State in November, 1917, there can be no doubt as to the political soundness of its arguments from history against legislative centralisation in so vast an area :—

"The examples of the United States, Canada, Australia and South Africa, as contrasted with India, China and the dependencies of Spain and France in the eighteenth century, prove that under elective institutions provincial administration cannot be made effective for units of population the size of great nations. Had the United States attempted to develop herself on the basis of five or six provinces, each would, for administrative reasons, have been driven to subdivide itself into minor self-governing provinces commensurate in size with the existing forty-eight States. County councils or district boards cannot take the place of provincial governments, which in nations of a certain magnitude, must be interposed between local authorities on the one hand, and the national government on the other. Hence, the Government of the United Kingdom, with its population of 45,000,000, is increasingly unable to cope with their need for social reform."

In a word, for India, with her vast population, her varied provinces and races, her many sectarian differences (brought to the surface by the present search for the lines of constitutional advance), a unilateral form of free government is impossible. If we include in our survey the far greater grouping of to-morrow, to which we have given the name of the South Asiatic Federation, the idea is still more hopelessly impracticable. It is common knowledge that, even with an administration not responsible to the people and an elaborate bureaucratic system, there have been increasing complaints by the Indian provincial administrations of excessive interference and of being kept in leading strings by the central authority. Masterful Viceroys like Lord Curzon have sought to keep all the threads of administration in their own hands ; but when their tenure has expired the provincial officials have renewed their efforts to modify and lessen the control of Simla. Diversified as have been the reform proposals submitted to Mr. Montagu during his Indian tour, there has been an extraordinary consensus of opinion that the growth in recent years of the activities of Government render imperative the devolution of some of the powers exercised by the central authority.

An outstanding difficulty in providing a central parliament for India is that the vast majority of the inhabitants are alike illiterate and in such deep poverty as to render impracticable their enfranchisement as electors of an Imperial assembly. Still, this argument should not be used by reactionaries, bureaucrats, and Anglo-Indians generally against the Indian educated classes in their plea for constitutional reform. It must not be forgotten that since the earliest years of the present century Indian leaders, under the inspiration of that lamented patriot G. K. Gokhale, have advocated universal and compulsory free education, in full recognition that its cost will have to be borne in some form or another by the taxpayers of the country. The claim for at least a beginning in this direction has been made by the National Congress since 1904. For reasons of a practical kind, which do not seem to me to have been adequate and which are steadily losing their force, officialdom did not see its way to make such a beginning even on a local option basis, until last year, when the Bombay Government supported the Bill of a non-official member which duly passed into law, for giving municipalities power to compel school attendance. It cannot be said that theories of the freedom of the individual and Spencerian ideas of limitation of State activity stood in the way. For, after all, the officials with whom the last word rested have been reared in a country where universal compulsory education has been established for more than forty-five years. The experiment has been tried with substantial success in some of the

Native States, under wise and patriotic princes like the rulers of Baroda, Bikaner, Mysore, Kapurthala, Cochin, and Bhavanagar. I do not deny the existence of practical difficulties in the application of the principle under the diversified conditions obtaining in the vast territories of British India; but with patient determination these can be steadily surmounted, and it seems to me that there is no strong reason for not giving general local option to confer this great boon on the people, other than the natural reluctance of an overwhelmingly non-indigenous administration to impose new taxation.

Wherever the blame may lie for the illiteracy of the masses, the fact remains that in the face of such ignorance and of the existence of interests so diversified and widely scattered, a central parliament becomes an impossibility. One cannot imagine the Baluch representative in an assembly at Delhi being keen on the needs of Madura, or a Bombay member advocating measures for the development of shipping in Calcutta. The well-known difficulties as to the representation of very small minorities also come in the way. While a mighty minority of many millions, like the Mahomedans, could protect its own interests in a central institution, the smallest and least influential communities, usually to be found in one province, could exert little or no influence at Delhi or Simla.

It should be remembered that the greatest political mistake in Indian annals was when Aurangzeb overthrew the independent states of the South and tried the impossible task of bringing the whole of India under Delhi. Historically, neither in Buddhist, Hindu, nor Mahomedan times has the entire peninsula been under one single government, and the actual India of to-day contains provinces that were never ruled by either Asoka or Akbar. And to their honour let it be said that, so far, the majority of Indian thinkers have advocated, if not the form, at least the facts of federal government. No doubt, the fear of seeing India again breaking up into component parts has made some Indian thinkers somewhat dubious as to the future under provincial autonomy. As the examples of the United States and Germany on the one hand, and of Russia on the other, have shown, the real danger of a break-up does not come from meeting the wishes of the different component parts, but from over-centralisation and the enforcement of an unnatural uniformity. No, the problem of a free India within the British Empire can only be solved by federalism and by facing this essential fact.

Of course no contemporary federal scheme can be followed in all its details ; there must be adaptation to Indian conditions and historical developments. Before going into details it should be observed that we must not be deflected from acceptance of certain broad principles of federalism because they happen to be applied in Germany, any more than we are called upon to adopt them because the United States of America are their earlier home. I yield to no one in the intense horror and detestation I feel in respect to the remorseless barbarity, the disregard of international obligations as to the rules of war, the treachery and trickery, and the enslavement of the inhabitants of conquered areas which have disgraced the German name in the last four years. But the political, like the theological, investigator should "seize the truth where'er 'tis found," whether in the the New World or the Old, and must not be blinded to the advantages of certain principles of confederation because they happen to have been applied in a country which has brought so much sorrow and suffering upon mankind.

The bursting of the floodgates of German lust of conquest was due, not to the constitution of her federal system, but to the arrogance and egotism instilled into her people, of set purpose, for a generation past. It is notorious that all classes, and not merely the military and ruling castes, were eager for war. They had grown rich in material things too quickly after the unification of the Empire, and acquired the aggressiveness characteristic of *nouveaux riches*. In the pre-war decade I frequently met middle-class Germans, not of the Junker class, but traders in India and Burma, in the Dutch Colonies, in Siam, China, Japan, America, in various parts of Africa, and on the Continent. They did not conceal their intense longing for war, and usually they blamed the weakness of the Kaiser, derisively calling him "the Pacifist." It is my firm conviction that if Germany had had a Government directly responsible to parliament and removable thereby, the war would have come several years sooner, and probably in 1906 over the question of Morocco.

Wherever we may look for patterns, I now propose to show that for some years to come each Indian province in the initial stages of federalism, must have a constitution that provides, on the one hand, for an independent and strong executive, responsible to the Viceroy and the Secretary of State for tenure of office and appointment; and, on the other hand, for elective assemblies to control finance and legislation. Thus will be built up the future United States of India within the British Empire. This system, leaving the component members of the federation full local autonomy, will best conform to the varied needs of the great peninsula and to the facts of her evolution, and can most readily be adjusted to local conditions.

CHAPTER IV

PROVINCIAL REORGANISATION

ANYONE acquainted with recent Indian political history is aware that nearly all suggested plans of constitutional reform are based on a greater or less degree of provincial autonomy. Lord Hardinge's Government, which included two warm champions of real devolution in the late Sir John Jenkins and Sir Ali Imam, laid down this principle in unequivocal terms in the famous Delhi despatch of 1911. Most of the outstanding and detailed reform proposals submitted to the Viceroy and Mr. Montagu last winter were based on the claim of provincial autonomy, at least over recognised and limited fields. This, too, was the keynote of Mr. Gokhale's political testament, which I had the privilege of publishing shortly before the announcement in the House of Commons of the liberalising policy of His Majesty's Government. Though it leaves the Governor-General in Council for the present great powers of intervention in the affairs of the local Governments, the Gokhale scheme was designed to lead, after a few years of practical working, to a form of federalism.

Though my lamented friend wrote out his plan only a few days before his death, he had long pondered deeply thereon, and had discussed the various points both with the late Sir P. M. Mehta and myself. He began expounding his ideas on this head to me in London in the early autumn of 1914. Recognising that the scheme led to federalism, I drew his attention to the consideration that the existing provinces had grown out of the accidents of foreign acquisition and the needs, many of them no longer operative, of bureaucratic administration ; in area, population, and still more potent matters of race and language, they were ill adapted to become national states. I proposed that he should found his scheme as far as possible on a plan of reshapement providing a national and linguistic basis. I said that self-government must develop on two lines, one being that of provincial rearrangement with something like the unity of a nationality as far as practicable, and the other the separate representation within each province of religions, castes, and communities, small as well as great. Gokhale agreed with this view, and his skeleton plan recognises the need for separate and direct representation of Mahomedans and other non-majority communities. But he did not feel justified in making provincial regrouping a part of his scheme, because he hoped that the Government would introduce, within a year or two from that date, the provincial autonomy foreshadowed in the Delhi despatch, and that its working, by bringing out the defects of present geographical divisions, would lead to the establishment of ethnic and linguistic groupings.

Now that the war has gone on not only months but years beyond the time Gokhale anticipated, even in his least optimistic hours, the currents of political progress to which men direct their gaze for the future have gained cumulative force, and the foundations to-day must be laid deep and strong. Happily, the task in India, if earnestly faced, does not present insuperable difficulties. I strongly oppose the suggested subdivision of the existing provinces into a considerable number of self-governing states. Such small administrations would unduly narrow down national effort. The unit of provincial self-government must be equal at least to a medium European state. It seems to me that in the Bengal Presidency we have a good example of a suitable and reasonably homogeneous area for federal autonomy. Nor would I divide so ethnically distinct a province as Burma. But in the other major provinces readjustment is necessary. Behar should absorb a few districts from the Central Provinces, and the United Provinces should take from what is now the Nagpur Government the Hindi-speaking districts which were formerly under the Agra Administration. On the other hand, two or three of the western districts of the United Provinces belong by affinity to the Punjab.

The Bombay Presidency as now constituted is unduly heterogeneous. With the disappearance of the Central Provinces the Marathi-speaking divisions would naturally fall to Bombay. The great Southern province of Madras would not be greatly changed, excepting that its most north-western districts would fall to Bombay, being nearer the Belgaum and North Kanara districts in character than to the Dravidian south. Bombay would lose Sind, which would substantially help to form what might be called the Indus Province, possibly with Quetta as the capital, and comprising the North-West Frontier Province as well as Baluchistan. Apart from Assam we should thus have eight "major" provinces, roughly equal in area, and each capable of developing a national government. It is true that in Bombay there would be the two main varieties of the original Sanskrit in the Marathi and Gujerati dialects; and in Madras Tamil and Telugu would similarly form the major languages. Everywhere beyond the areas where it is the principal vernacular Urdu would be the recognised home tongue of the Mahomedans. But these and other linguistic variations are inevitable in a subcontinent so diversified as India; and by such a scheme of redistribution there would be much greater approximation than at present to provinces which could honestly be called nationalities, each having an importance and coherence ranking with those of at least some European States.

The Governor of each province should directly represent the Sovereign and hold all official executive responsibility. His powers, while similar to those now vested in the heads of presidencies, would be much larger and far less trammelled by the central authority in India. The appointment would be made, as at present, by the King-Emperor. In one important respect I dissent from most of the systems which have been proposed, for I consider the time has come for including Indians within the field of selection. I grant that there are not many Indians who could fitly hold this exalted office in the reconstituted form; but a beginning could and should be made. The arguments used by Lord Morley a decade ago in wearing down the opposition to appointing Indians to the Government of India and the presidency Executives, may be applied to this claim that, in conformity with the great principles of Queen

Victoria's Proclamation of 1858, Indians should now preside over provinces side by side with Englishmen.

The innovation should be made by inviting one of the ruling princes to leave his own territory for five years for the greater field of direction of a provincial administration. To take a concrete case, there is no reason why that patriot-statesman the Maharaja of Bikanir should not succeed Lord Pentland or Lord Willingdon. There are certainly other ruling princes capable of administrating great provinces; but I take His Highness of Bikanir as a shining example, whose qualifications cannot be denied. As to the objection that five years is too long a period for any prince to leave his own territory, it may be answered that a well-run Native State reaches such a degree of automatic good administration that, when its ruler dies, the standard is maintained during long periods of regency. Moreover, nowadays there are usually either heirs-apparent or other relatives of the ruler who could well be trusted to carry on the administration for a quinquennium.

During the period the selected ruling chief would undergo a personal metamorphosis; but I am confident that our best modern princes are quite capable of adapting themselves to such a change of situation. They will be able to play their new part and take up their wider responsibilities, exactly as an Englishman forgets that he is a large landowner in Kent or Surrey when he becomes a governor or ambassador. On a small scale something of the kind occurred when the gallant Maharaja Sir Partab Singh abdicated the Idar *gadi*, and returned to Jodhpur to be regent for his grand-nephew. The English heads of neighbouring provinces would find substantial advantage in the contiguity of an Indian ruler of proved administrative ability, dealing with public problems corresponding to his own. Later on ordinary British Indian subjects should be eligible for appointment to governorships; but for some years to come the great responsibility should be limited to Indian princes. It may be undesirable to appoint a ruling chief to the governorship of the province in which his State is situated; but there is no reason why a prince from Rajputana or Central India should not make an excellent head of the Executive in Bengal, Bombay, or Madras.

The Governor should appoint ministers to the various departments of State, for defined periods of, say, four or five years at least, and his choice should be unhampered. Except in the peculiar Helvetian Confederation, no Prime Minister or President in the world has to accept his colleagues at the bidding of an electorate or the legislature. Nor is the exception absolute: for when a federal councillor or minister has been elected, his tenure of office does not depend upon any vote of the Swiss Parliament. The world-wide practice whereby the head of the administration selects his colleagues is based on historical experience, and must be maintained in India. By way of safeguard, however, the legislature might possess the right of removing by a three-fourths majority, an unsuitable or incompetent man at the head of a department. Apart from this minor and negative degree of legislative control, each minister should be entirely responsible to the Crown through the Governor. This would give India the constitution Gokhale and Mehta always advocated, on the basis of the American or the German principle of freedom of the executive from legislative control so far as tenure of office is concerned. An adverse vote would only lead to the dropping of the measure in hand.

The greatest mistake made in the successive reconstitutions of Indian provincial legislatures has been that of limiting the right of representation, in practice if not always in theory, to what may be termed the privileged classes—the best-educated and richest sections of the population. Owing to this serious error the national conservatism necessary to the evolution of a normal modern State, and in India characteristic of the man at the plough, has been artificially prevented from making its voice effectively heard. An exaggerated mid-Victorian form of Liberalism, natural to the classes that now form the narrow electorates, has been dominant. Taxation and representation have not gone together. The provincial legislatures have been far too small to be really representative bodies in such large areas. I am sure an able and popular Governor, such as Lord Willingdon in Bombay, could rule his province much better if he had an assembly of from 180 to 220 almost entirely elected members, instead of about one-fifth of that number nominated and elected, as now, for it could then be representative of every district, community and substantial interest.

Each of the various religions and races, as recorded in the census, would provincially be a *millet*, to use the Turkish term, and each would have a fair share in the assembly directly elected. The franchise might be based on various grounds—a small income or land tax assessment, public service, both civilian and military, education and other tests. Old soldiers of a prescribed period of service, especially all who have participated in the present war, men who in various capacities have travelled far out of India, and those who have served in important posts would have special qualifications for the franchise, but each within his own community. There would still remain large numbers of the less fortunate classes and castes who could not at present be fairly represented, since they do not include any substantial proportion of men with such educational or other qualifications as to pass the reasonable tests applied to other sections. For the present, therefore, it should be the duty of the Governor to nominate a few representatives from these backward communities.

Such an assembly, though falling short of the wide bases of such outstanding types as the House of Commons or the French Chamber, would have the merit of truly reflecting Indian conditions of to-day. I am not advocating an institution for twenty or thirty years hence, but one that could safely and advantageously be introduced without delay, since it would be calculated to strengthen the Executive and promote the contentment of all classes. A natural organic epitome of existing conditions, it would grow, as all healthy political institutions have grown, till it reached a standard similar to that built up stage by stage in the best-governed parts of the world. Since Mahomedans and the land-owning classes received special representation under the Morley reforms, and as a matter of practical politics it is impossible to force the Mahomedan to surrender these rights, this principle must be extended, both on logical and political grounds, to other important communities and interests. This extension would meet the claims, so strongly pressed within the last year or so, of the non-Brahmans of Madras, and of the British and Anglo-Indian communities, as well as of other minority elements, and would stimulate an interest in public affairs on the part of the backward classes.

While the Assembly, apart from the three-fourths vote of censure by which it could remove individual ministers, would not otherwise control the Executive, it would have full powers within its legitimate sphere of influence. But single Chamber government is to be deprecated, and I strongly advocate the establishment in each province of a Senate or Upper House, of, say, forty or fifty members. Here again, for the present, nomination would be exercised in some instances, while in other cases important bodies or interests, such as the greater municipalities, chambers of commerce, universities, and landlords' associations, would send representatives. Europeans sojourning for long periods in India for commercial or professional purposes would have direct representation in the larger Chamber, and indirect representation in the Upper House. The two Houses, in case of difference of opinion, would vote together as a united assembly, and the point at issue would be decided by a majority. The second Chamber should be constituted *pari passu* with the reconstitution of the existing legislature.

The power of the two Houses over legislation and provincial finance should be subject only to the veto of the Governor. But provincial finance and its sources of revenue will have to be carefully marked out, since the present system whereby the Government of India, or rather the Secretary of State, is the ultimate disposer of these revenues must disappear. At the same time, as a later chapter will show, care must be taken to leave the character of the Government of India sufficiently elastic to provide for ultimate and natural development from a purely British-Indian to a fully South Asiatic federal administration. Once we have the provinces based on nationality, worked out as described, we can well leave them a full measure of self-government for their internal affairs, such as applies to the greater Native States, for example, Hyderabad or Mysore. There would be little for the central Government to interfere with, and that little would be statutorily restricted as time went on.

An objection to be met is that since separate representation may strengthen centrifugal tendencies it is inconsistent with the general language and race bases of provincial readjustment. The answer is that we must legislate to meet actual rather than ideal conditions. The various religions, communities, castes, et cetera, within each great province have very much in common, something national in effort and aspiration, that will meet the difficulty of separate communal representation in practical working and in time. On the other hand, the smaller communities by being assured from the first of their voice in affairs will feel growing confidence in the autonomous system, and the self-respect and self-confidence so necessary to the backward classes in India will steadily grow. There will be awakened in them an enthusiasm for great public interests that now lies dormant, and an increasing fellow-feeling with the leading communities.

A few years' experience of this system would go far to satisfy the crying needs of India. The diversified problems of education, sanitation, public works, commerce and industry would be solved by each State in a natural, healthy way. Each would develop itself sufficiently to become an independent and worthy member of the great South Asiatic Federation destined to take its place by the side of the other dominions within the Empire of the King.

CHAPTER V

THE PROTECTED STATES

NO federal scheme for India can be complete or satisfactory if it leaves out of account the Native States, which cover one-third of the area of the Indian Empire and contain some seventy million inhabitants, or two-ninths of the entire population. It is therefore necessary to deal with them before discussing the constitution of the central authority.

It is a familiar though often forgotten fact that these principalities vary in size, climate, density of population, economic, racial, and intellectual conditions to an extraordinary degree. There are great dominions, such as Hyderabad, Mysore, and Kashmir, worthy to rank with kingdoms in Europe. The Nizam of Hyderabad is the equal in power, in dominion, in the number of his subjects, and in the variety of interests to be considered, with the Kings of Belgium or Roumania. Indeed, just as the German Emperor has kings within his dominions, and as we hope some day the independent sovereigns of Persia and Afghanistan will, of their own free will, wish to enter the future South Asiatic Confederation, so, prima facie, there is every reason why the Nizam should, like the former Kings of Oudh, receive the royal title of "Majesty," a concomitant act being the rendition to him of the

Berars. A step forward was taken on New Year's Day, 1918, when he was given the special title of "Faithful Ally of the British Government," and the style, new to India, of "His Exalted Highness." This designation is strangely reminiscent of the old Dutch style of "High Mightiness," which was proposed for the President of the United States, but refused by Washington.

Then there are States not so vast in extent where, by intensive culture, commerce and trade have reached such a development as to make them the equals of the richest British districts in India. Some of the principalities go back in tradition and history to the very dawn of civilised society. There are Rajput States, the germs of which must have existed when Alexander encamped on the banks of the Indus, and it is not improbable that orderly governments, under the ancestors or collaterals of some of the present Rajput princes, were carried on in the eras of Cæsar and Augustus. Other principalities, again, date in present form from the early days of British rule, and in some cases were obtained by purchase or by other equally unromantic forms of acquisition from English officials, reluctant to accept further direct responsibility for Indian government. But whether ancient or comparatively new, the individual variations of these autonomous territories are of absorbing interest. Large dominions, like those of Baroda and Gwalior, possess a unity of history and sentiment attaching them to their ruling houses, from which, especially in the case of their present heads, they have received such devoted service as to have established between prince and people a relation almost tribal in the strength of its affection. There are smaller States, such as Kapurthala and Bhavanagar, which are excellent examples of hereditary good government and contentment of the people.

Amid the diversities I have indicated, there is an all-embracing link of profound attachment to the British Crown. Not only through this vast war, but on many previous occasions, in almost every frontier expedition, in China, in Africa, and elsewhere, the princes have proved their devotion to the British Empire, and have made sacrifices such as to win for them the merited title of partners therein. In the last four years they have been enabled, by freewill gifts and sacrifices, to share in the great task of securing a victory for the Allies to an extent which has evoked general admiration and has vastly raised the scale of India's contribution as a whole. Their well-trained Imperial Service contingents, maintained by the Durbars for a generation past, formed an invaluable contribution to the military units in being when war broke out, and the stream of recruitment from the States has enormously helped to meet the pressing need for repair of the heavy wastages of war.

Looking back on the 150 years of British predominance in India, I can see scarcely any other act equal alike in wisdom, justice, and far-sightedness, to Queen Victoria's promise through Canning, on the morrow of the Mutiny, to refrain from the absorption of any Native States into British India. It came to relieve the fears and anxieties aroused, with unhappy results, by the Dalhousian policy of "lapse." Had that policy been vetoed at the time by the Government in Whitehall, I am firmly convinced that Britain's position in India to-day would have been all the stronger, for the existence of

Oudh, Nagpur, Satara, and the other sequestered principalities. The aggregate territory from which British Indian revenues are derived would have been less vast, and I do not deny that there would have been some other disadvantages, of a temporary character, but these would have been altogether outweighed. The administrative machinery of British India, now so great and cumbrous, would have been simplified; British rule would have had in those directly concerned sure and honest friends like the princes of to-day, and there would have been a correspondingly larger measure of indigenous government, with all its advantages, side by side with British administration. The builders of United Germany, from Bismarck downwards, have borne witness that the diversified principalities are the mainstay of that Empire, and that destructive anarchy has no more powerful antagonist than a dynasty belonging to the soil, ruling from age to age relatively small areas within a confederation.

It is not too much to say that to-day the Indian princes are the bulwarks of the Imperial connection. I have sometimes met Indians whose names, of course, I can never mention even in private, actuated by bitter hatred of England, and whose absorbing idea was to cut the painter. On one point they were all agreed: that the existence of the Native States made an insuperable barrier to the success of their childish ambition, and it was always with bitter regret that they referred to these principalities.

From the point of view of good administration these areas of indigenous rule, scattered like so many islands of varying size in the sea of British

India, are advantageous both to their own inhabitants and to those of surrounding districts. They provide suitable fields for administrative experiments such as could not be applied, without prior test, to the whole of British India. Some States advance the cause of social reform by enactments and orders which English administrators, conscious of their limitations as non-indigenous officials adhering to the principle of strict religious neutrality, have not dared to apply. In some services for the commonweal, such as education and sanitation, there are respects in which the most progressive States are ahead of British India. But it would be unfair to fail to recognise that the stimulus to advancement is reciprocal. The high standard of British justice, to give but one instance, calls for emulation, as is recognised by almost every State. Here and there are to be found principalities in which the administration of justice and general civil policy leave much to be desired ; but happily, with the spread of modern ideals, these have become rare exceptions. Religious liberty prevails in the States as well as in British India. A Moslem ruler, like the Nizam of Hyderabad, is respected and loved by his millions of Hindu subjects, while there are Hindu Princes, such as the Maharajas of Gwalior and Kolahpur (to mention only two names), whose Mahomedan subjects look upon them with almost filial affection and veneration, and who constantly prove that, if Hindus in faith, they are superior as rulers to all sectarian or other narrowing influences.

Again, these indigenous Courts scattered over the great peninsula are the fitting patrons of art in every form. Indian music, architecture, painting, and the arts generally, have natural protectors and patrons in the various Durbars. It is not improbable that within the present century some of the dynasties may produce patrons of art as influential as the Medicis, or the princes of Weimar. Some special branches of higher agriculture receive encouragement from the princes, and in many other directions they give a remarkable impetus to the upbuilding of an expanded Indian life, responsive to modern ideas yet distinctive of the country and its peoples.

Increasingly, of late years, some of the best-known princes have been cherishing the ideal of a constitutional and parliamentary basis for their administrations. There can be no doubt that a liberal policy in British India will soon be followed in many of the States by widening applications of the principle of co-operation between the rulers and the ruled. It is most gratifying to Indian patriots to note the sympathy which the princes and nobles have shown with the aspirations of the people of British India toward self-government. After all, these rulers, unlike the small dynasties of the eighteenth and nineteenth centuries in Italy, are children of the soil and have a natural sympathy and fellow-feeling with their countrymen.

There could be no better or more convincing presentation of these aspirations of India, in brief compass, than that given by the Maharaja of Bikanir, in his historic pronouncement at the luncheon of the Empire Parliamentary Association to the Indian delegates to the Imperial War Conference, at the House of Commons, on 24th April, 1917. Those of us who personally know the ruling princes of to-day—so active, hardworking, patriotic, and devoted to the welfare of their people, usually so free from all "side," and, in a word, so different from the legendary maharaja of the imaginative writers of the past—have no reason to doubt that this eloquent plea voiced not only the views of the educated people of India but also those of the average ruling chief. In fact, His Highness of Bikanir spoke on similar lines to his brother princes when they entertained him to dinner in Bombay on the eve of his departure for the Imperial War Conference. It may also be noted that the Maharaja of Alwar's speeches, so full of democratic enthusiasm, have made a considerable impression in India within the last two or three years.

The States cannot be mere spectators of the constitutional changes now impending. The question arises, "What is the part they are to play in the politically free India of to-morrow?" To reduce them gradually to the mere position of great nobles, and to let the power and the individuality attaching to their States pass out of their control would be a crime against history, art, and even nationality. On the other hand, the present standard of relations between the protecting Power and the protected State cannot go on after British India reaches the first stages toward self-government. What is the solution? Happily in federalism we find a system that will meet the need both of British India and of the Native States. It has been maintained in these pages that a successful unilateral form of self-government is impossible even for British India. The great provincial administrations, we have seen, must be autonomous in internal matters. The interference of the central authority, while necessary in the past, must be metamorphosed into that entire non-intervention in State as distinct from Imperial affairs which characterises the Imperial Government of Germany or the United States Government in their dealings with the members of their respective confederations. A similar policy should at once be applied to the Indian principalities. In the succeeding chapter we shall show that the fact that these States are of such varying sizes and importance is not a bar to their incorporation in the proposed federal system.

CHAPTER VI

THE CENTRAL GOVERNMENT

AS previously indicated, after the grant of autonomy to each newly constituted national State the Government of India would retain temporarily powers of general control over the provincial administrations. But this would be only for the purpose of carrying out with each province individually the various conventions by which authority over the whole series of legislation, finance, and administration comprehended in the term " Home Affairs " would be completely transferred to the constitutional bodies previously described, with the Governor possessing a veto over legislation and finance. If an Assembly rejected the annual budget, the Governor would be entitled to carry on with a repetition of the previous year's financial policy and the existing taxes, as in Japan and Austria.

While, on the one hand, the conventions would assure Home Rule to the State administrations, on the other hand, they would conserve to the central authority those Imperial and federal powers without which the confederacy would go to pieces. We have the historical fact of the existence of major Native States, such as Hyderabad, with treaty rights; and such internal powers as are vested in the Nizam's Government should be exercised by the provincial States. Of the departments retained by the central Government, the first and foremost would be those of close relationship with the Imperial Government in London, through the Secretary of State for India. His position would more and more approximate to that of the Secretary of State for the Colonies, and his Council would be abolished. The right now exercised by the Presidency Governments to correspond with the Secretary of State on certain matters would apply to all the national States; though naturally the interest of the British Cabinet would be much greater in those branches of the administration which would fall to the central Government. Prominent amongst them would be foreign affairs. By this I do not mean relations with the Native States, which are now part of the work of the Foreign department at Delhi, but with external countries, including such future States as may be drawn hereafter within the orbit of the confederation through their own freewill and interest.

The Army and Navy would naturally belong to the central Government, and so would maritime affairs generally, including customs. Here some sacrifice on the part of certain Native States will be necessary, for just as the central Government would cede to the provincial authorities all those branches of internal business now administered by the principalities, so the principalities, in conjunction with the provincial States, would have to accept full military and naval and customs control by the Government of India. But this need not interfere with the sentimental connection of each State with its contingent to the Imperial Army. While full control of promotion, brigading, et cetera, would remain in the hands of the central authority, the contingents raised in Native States would carry symbols of their origin, and the princes would be honorary commanders of their respective corps. Apart from customs, the Government of India would receive a settled contribution from each province. In the case of Native States the old and rather humiliating "tribute" paid in some instances, and now amounting to about £617,000, would be abolished and replaced by a uniform percentage of contribution equal to that paid by the provincial States. Public works and sanitation would belong to each province, but railway administration and finance, with uniformity or fair adjustment of rates over the whole extent of the federation, would be a branch of Imperial government.

This system would possess the great advantage of enabling the most progressive provinces to go ahead in their social legislation, without being restricted, as would often be the case under a uniform system, to the pace of the slowest and most backward. In an all-India legislature a project of social reform, such as Mr. Bupendranath Basu's Civil Marriage Bill, is almost inevitably judged from the point of view of the provinces least prepared for the advance. Under this scheme of federation education in all its branches, social laws (such as those of succession and marriage), control over the building of tenements and conditions of labour, agricultural improvements, scientific research and medical aid—progress in all these vital interests would become a matter of healthy competition. Each province, while able to adapt its policy to local conditions, would be stirred to do its utmost to lead in the race for political and social development. No longer cribb'd, cabin'd, and confined by the central secretariats, the advanced parts of the country, such as Bombay or Bengal, may be expected to reach a standard of social polity that will be a beacon light for the other provinces to follow.

The headship of the Government of India would naturally remain with the representative of the King-Emperor, the Viceroy, to whose position the next chapter is devoted. Then would come his Cabinet, presided over by the Prime Minister, and containing members for Defence, Finance and Customs, Railways, External Commerce, Foreign Affairs, and two Ministers for the Interior. One of these would have charge of all relations with the federated authorities, and the other would deal with the judicial, legal, constitutional, and other branches of federal affairs not otherwise provided for. Here again the principle of selection for the Cabinet proposed for the provincial administrations would apply. The Prime Minister, under the Viceroy's guidance, would choose his colleagues without restraint as he thought best.

In what is now known as the Imperial Legislature the most radical change will be inevitable. For the short transitional period before the Government of India relinquishes detailed control of the provinces, a strong central legislature, with special representation of the various provinces and races, to help with the conventions, will be necessary. But after the due establishment of the federal constitution, the room for Imperial legislation and as distinct from questions of policy, will be so restricted that my preference is for a Senate or

Council, representing the provinces and the Native States, instead of needlessly complicating the federal organisation by the creation of two central chambers, with little to legislate about.

To this body each of the great provinces should send eight to ten representatives, some chosen by the Governor and approved by either one or the other House, and the remainder selected by each of the Assemblies and approved by the Governor. The great States like Kashmir, Mysore, or Gwalior would send five representatives, and Hyderabad, as the premier State, seven; and even the smallest States whose ruler is included in the table of salutes would have at least one member. As in the German constitution, where the Federal Council safeguards the interests of every member of the Bundesrat by giving to the smallest representation far above its numerical proportion, so here the medium States, such as Bikanir and Patiala, would have two or three representatives, coming down to at least one member for such principalities as Janjira or Morvi.

The Senate would legislate for the whole of India when necessary; but the proposed federal constitution will make such occasions rare or formal. They would ordinarily be confined to measures such as the Defence of India Act, or dealing with the protection of the coast, or tariffs, or Army and Navy services. The Government of India, in exercise of full fiscal autonomy, would establish for the entire federation the necessary tariffs with scientific schedules. The English Liberal, with his traditional mistrust of tariffs, too often forgets how totally different is the case of India from that of his own country. He knows that in England

Protection would mean, in practice, mainly a tax on corn, and result in raising the cost of various foodstuffs for the poorest classes. Her dependence on exterior supplies has been most pointedly demonstrated by the submarine campaign. In India, on the contrary, the food of the people is home grown, and a very considerable surplus remains for shipment abroad; the imports consist to a great extent of articles of luxury or such manufactured articles as can safely be taxed in order to encourage indigenous industry.

Under the new order of things the atmosphere of Simla or Delhi should be serene and dispassionate. The Government of India would be the connecting bond between great national provinces and principalities, united for common purposes but varying in organic and natural unity, representing their diversified history, races, religions, and languages. They would be not like to like, but like in difference:

> Not chaos like together crushed and bruised,
> But, like the world, harmoniously diffused,
> Where order in variety we see,
> And where, though all may differ, all agree.

The central federal authority, by promoting happiness, contentment, and development within its vast territories and over such an immense population, would sooner or later attract its neighbours in Northern and Western Asia. The benefits of federalism would soon be felt, since it would give a stimulus to progress which present conditions of centralisation discourage and retard. At the periodical Imperial Conferences in London, the representatives of Canada, Australia, and the other great Dominions, would meet those who would voice the claims of an immense Indian Federation built on the rock of national autonomy in each of its living members. They would represent an organic whole which, in very truth, would be a living and vital entity with common interests, looked after by a federal Government and a strong Imperial Executive supervised by the Emperor's representative, the Viceroy, and his Prime Minister and Cabinet, and supported by the Federal Council representing all provinces and principalities.

CHAPTER VII

THE VICEROYALTY

IT is an accepted principle of modern statesmanship that the nation or federation of nations should be as broadly based as circumstances permit upon the opinion of the people, that the larger and more varied the foundations of the national life are made, the stronger will be the body politic. The Reform Act of 1918, enfranchising women and adding millions of men to the British electorate, notwithstanding the probability of mistakes here and there under the influence of these new elements, is yet certain to increase the strength of the realm by giving large numbers a personal and direct interest in the public welfare. Even the governing classes of Prussia and its Court, whose sympathy with democracy is merely opportunist, have come to the conclusion that by the conferment of manhood suffrage the Constitution and the monarchy will gain strength rather than lose it. In India, under the system proposed in these pages, the suffrage will be as wide as is reasonably practicable. Hundreds of thousands of the people will gain a new sense of responsibility in public affairs, and will be stimulated to take an active interest in the internal administration of the country.

While such widening of the base is essential, we must not overlook the importance of the apex.

Without unity of influential guidance national life is inevitably wanting in organic energy. But in searching for the apex of society, as in searching for a reformed Constitution, we must be guided by the history, the character, and the experience of the nation or race. The Presidency of the United States is a fine example of a naturally evolved institution in keeping with the conditions of the soil. But for India, for manifold historical, racial, and even religious reasons, the monarchy can be the only ultimate apex. In spite of innumerable differences of race, character, and psychology, in a very real sense (certainly as real as the claim of episcopal succession from St. Peter made by the Roman and Anglican Churches) our King-Emperor is in the line of succession from Asoka and Chandragupta.

This is so because from time immemorial, in periods of peace and happiness, India has had in practice its federal sovereigns and its over-lord. It is true that the ancient Hindu monarchy and society had become so weakened a millennium ago and more (probably owing to India's geographical isolation from the then world movements) that in the successive waves of Mahomedan invasion from the North the ancient polity was overthrown. For a long time thereafter Hindu and Moslem political history in India reveals an unconscious attempt on the part of dynasties, principalities, and nations to recreate the common Empire which had been dissolved long before. The men of genius among the Afghan and other dynasties that "had their day and ceased to be" obviously searched for a constitution that would leave local power in the hands of the many rajas, and yet unite their forces for common effort under the central power at Delhi.

Akbar at last, in part by his own military and administrative genius (as carefully shown in Mr. Vincent Smith's lately published critical biography), but infinitely more owing to the working of eight hundred years of historical causes, re-established the position of national emperor. Innumerable national, dynastic, racial, and historical factors culminated in the Great Mogul; but even under his rule seeds were sown that led to a disintegration as widespread as any that took place before his day. It was perhaps inevitable that this ambitious conqueror should over-centralise; but his two much less able successors carried that policy still further. Even the judicious policy of marrying Hindu princesses encouraged the tendency, for many of the rajas whose families had thus become matrimonially linked with the splendid Court of Delhi gradually sunk into the position of nobles instead of retaining that of federal allies.

With Aurangzeb the policy of excessive centralisation culminated. The foolish conquest of the Southern kingdoms, and not religious bigotry, was the real cause of his prolonged conflict with the Hindus of the Deccan. Had he been content to leave the rich kingdoms of Bijapur and Golconda unannexed, it is probable that one of two things would have happened, each equally satisfactory from the point of view of Imperial consolidation. Either the Moslem dynasties of the South would have identified themselves more and more with their Hindu subjects, much as the early Nizams did, and ultimately the Southern kingdoms would have been federated with the empire-nation at Delhi. The other eventuality, that of the Mahrattas under Sivaji wiping away the local dynasties, would still have meant the establishment of a powerful confederacy in the South, but with a natural and inevitable attraction toward the empire of the North. Sooner or later, they would have united for common purposes, while each kept its own internal independence and national character. After careful study of Indian history from the rise of Akbar onwards, I have no hesitation in attributing the break-up of the Mogul Empire and the terrible anarchy of the eighteenth century mainly to the centralising policy of Akbar, Jehangir, Shah Jehan, and Aurangzeb.

I do not suggest that the alternative policy of leaving the principalities independent and bringing about a federal system would have relieved India of internal differences, wars, and complications, any more than it did the Holy Roman Empire of approximately the same period; but I hold that national greatness and freedom would have been maintained. There were not in India, as in Europe, two strong states and dynasties like Prussia and Austria, the Hohenzollerns and the Hapsburgs, to fight a hundred battles till one of them was turned out of the Empire, to return later to the ancient fold, but as an ally. There was no danger that India would see any such drama on her soil as the long-drawn tragedy of which the last act was played at Sadowa. The Moguls were the strongest and best organised of the forces existing in the peninsula, and in the pursuit of a federal policy they would have drawn around them, as planets, the Deccan States and Bengal, the principalities of Rajputna, and the newly born nationality of Afghans.

Fate decreed otherwise. From the death of Aurangzeb to the close of the eighteenth century the history of India is among the blackest in the annals of modern times. For all effective purposes the Mogul Empire had passed away. Hence Nadir Shah or Ahmed Shah Abdali could ravish the beautiful provinces of the North, kill Hindu and Moslem alike, and fritter away wealth and resources they could not but abuse. The tragedy of the triangular rivalry and bloodshed of Sikh, Hindu, and Moslem, so useless and insensate, in the Punjab, has never been painted by a capable historian in the dark colours it deserves. The Kings of Oudh, incompetent and ever looking to foreign alliances for support, destroyed the unity of a province designed by nature to be the right arm of the Empire. Disunited Bengal was the theatre of internecine war until the East India Company, obtaining the Dewani, established absolute and, at that time, by no means too benevolent rule. The southern half of India was degenerating into a vast jungle with the Pindari and the Mahratta ravaging provinces and states in all directions. Amid all this internal unrest the long-drawn contest of various European Powers for supremacy went on, and in particular the English and the French made the South the battleground for the settlement of their European differences.

Still the forces of ordered progress, so dear to the heart of mankind, were triumphant. In spite of a hundred checks and many errors, in spite of individual acts of harshness and injustice that no impartial student can deny, Britain raised India to the status of a great empire. As centuries of disorder and division had led to ultimate union under Akbar, so the generations of disaster and disintegration that followed the decay of the Mogul Empire led by imperceptible degrees to the union of India under Great Britain. That union has grown ever closer till to-day, in a sense more real than Akbar ever reached, George V is the successor of Asoka. In the British dynasty we have an imperial apex of Indian rule historically suited to the soil. The latter half of the nineteenth century was characterised by the constantly growing attachment of the people of India to the British Sovereign. Victoria, in the course of her long reign, came nearer to the hearts of the Indian subjects she loved so well than any of the Emperors the great peninsula had had in the last thousand years of her chequered history.

The many princes who visited the Court of Windsor during Her Majesty's reign took back to their territories, both personally and through their entourage, memories of her sincere and maternal affection for her Indian subjects. Her kindness and consideration towards such ordinary Indians as came near the presence, her employment of Indian personal servants, the pains she took to acquire a working knowledge of Hindostani—all this became widely known and appreciated in India. Peasants whom no one would credit with such knowledge often surprised Indians of education by their shrewd remarks on the Good Queen's affection for their country. The many years the Duke of Connaught spent in high military command in India, making friends everywhere, getting known to and learning to understand the people, wove further personal links with the Sovereign. The visits, first of the late King Edward when Prince of Wales, and later of the Duke of Clarence, were welcome reminders of the interest of the Royal Family in the country and its peoples.

This sentiment of attachment to the Crown, so consonant with Indian tradition and religious belief, has come to still fuller fruition under our present gracious Sovereign, who is as well known to and as well beloved by his Indian subjects as any emperor could desire. His first visit to India, as Prince of Wales, with its message of Sympathy, and still more his second visit as regnant Emperor, with its message of Hope, are ever near and dear memories to the hearts of the people. The Great War, with its community of sacrifice and suffering, with the ready and unfailing example of patriotic service and self-denial set by the monarch, and the evidences of his deep personal interest in the Indian troops in every theatre of conflict, has deepened and extended this great personal influence of the Royal House. The many Indian princes, gentlemen, soldiers, and others who have had the privilege of coming into contact with His Majesty —and their number has been much increased during the war—have been so many means of communion between the Emperor and his Eastern dominion. The feeling that, after all, India is not governed on the inconceivable theory of her vast conglomerate population being subject to another race, thousands of miles away, but owns allegiance to her own Emperor, is a unifying source of strength. The monarchy is the natural and fitting apex to the political structure, and must remain so amid all coming permutations. To cold casuists, hair-splitting in their studies, the Indian feeling of warm affection for the Sovereign may seem illogical; but it is one of the great formative forces of the world.

The Viceroy is the only direct representative of the Sovereign in the country. At the same time he is Prime Minister, the head of the executive, the authority to whom the provincial Governors and Lieutenant-Governors appeal for direction and counsel, the president of the Supreme Legislature, the Foreign Minister, and the chief connecting link with His Majesty's Government in Whitehall. He has so many other duties and heavy responsibilities that it is impossible for him, however great his capacities, to provide more than a relatively small proportion of the benefits derivable, either for England or for India, from the position of the Emperor's direct representative. The ordinary newspaper accounts of Viceregal doings and speeches are sufficient to show that the Governor-Generalship, the headship of the Executive, absorbs the major part of the Viceroy's time and thought. While in common parlance he is always known by the latter designation, it is not used in the warrant of appointment issued by the Crown, although in Royal Proclamations both titles are expressed. The standard official authority tells us that the title of Viceroy "appears to be one of ceremony, which may most appropriately be used in connection with the state and social functions of the Sovereign's representative." [1]

With the establishment of any federal constitution, a great change must come over the work of the Viceroy in any case. The time and thought

[1] *The Imperial Gazetteer of India*, Vol. IV, p. 16.

now given to the supervision of provincial administration must be directed more fully to strictly Imperial affairs. Ought not the opportunity to be taken to make a still more radical change, with the object of no longer leaving undeveloped the signal powers for good of the attachment of the people to the Royal House? If the political head of the federal Government at Delhi or Simla is to maintain a united Cabinet and promote a common policy, why should not India accept the experience of every other part of the world that a Prime Minister cannot also successfully play the rôle of viceroyalty?

These considerations, and the natural desire to make permanent the unifying bond of attachment to the Royal House, lead to the conclusion that the time has come to appoint to the viceregency a son or brother of the Sovereign, and to make the tenure non-political. The Royal representative would have his Prime Minister nominated at the same time, and for the same period of five years or so, by the Imperial Government in England; and the Viceroy and the Prime Minister would choose their British and Indian colleagues of the Cabinet. The only argument seriously advanced against appointing a member of the Royal Family as a non-political Viceroy when this suggestion was definitely made by myself [1] and others a dozen years ago was that the field for his activities would be insufficient to justify the additional expenditure. This pseudo-reasoning sounds strange from the lips of Britons who have become so familiar for generations with the benevolent activity and

[1] "Some Thoughts on the Indian Discontent," *National Review*, February, 1907.

unifying influence of a non-political and nation-representing monarch. An examination of only a few of the many advantages of this change will suffice to show that the argument is not only unsound in itself, but starts from a false premise.

In the first place, there would constantly be at the disposal of federal princes and the heads of federal provinces, of the Prime Minister and the members of the Cabinet, as a source of reference and advice, a socially superior, an independent mind, kept informed under the Constitution of all important events and policies, and with the right of advising, warning, and suggesting. These are great and beneficent powers, as is proved by the published *Letters of Queen Victoria*, 1837–1861, and by many biographies of the statesmen of her reign. There would be a second and constant mental influence, detached from direct participation in the controversies of the moment, able to throw a new light on the current problems of politics for the benefit of the Ministry. Since the control of Whitehall, now extending to small details, would be replaced to a considerable extent by that of the representatives of the States, provincial and indigenous, and, in the domain of Imperial finance, by that of the Federal Senate, there would be still greater need than at present of a permanent representative of the Throne, watching, advising, and, if things went wrong, warning. The position of the prince would raise him above all temptation or suspicion of any such motive as ambition for a great political future in the Parliamentary arena at home, and he would be looked to as the final judge and arbiter of the most important elements in inter-state relations, namely, those of good taste and good behaviour.

Another consideration has to be urged. We have seen that, in accordance with the principle Parliament laid down no less than eighty-five years ago, if a position can be worthily held by an Indian, he should not be debarred therefrom merely on grounds of race. Hence we have urged that appointments to provincial Governorships should not be beyond their reach. Can it honestly be maintained that there are no minds or characters in modern India equal to those of the Viceroys sent out from England? In intellect and character a Bikanir or a Sinha yield to none. If the Viceroyalty is to remain anything less than a constitutional rôle, a position due like the monarchy it represents to the symbolic power of hereditary kingship, then it must be open to Indians as well as Englishmen. No self-respecting Indian will allow for a moment mere racial superiority as an argument for the exclusion of his countrymen.

Then there is the immense and almost untilled field of individual social reform, of charity, and of social effort, which cannot be compassed by our present system of political viceroyalties with their absorbing duties. To take only a few instances: do Indian hospitals secure all the encouragement and supervision they merit? In the widest sense of the term, does not social help—not indeed from race to race or from class to class but from individual to individual—need organisation and encouragement? The seed which the Dowager Lady Dufferin and Lady Hardinge, to name but two Vicereines, steadfastly sowed in India has reached but an infinitesimal growth in comparison both with the need and the possibilities. In all such matters the successive occupants of Viceregal Lodge, Simla, have done their best; but the conditions render impossible close attention to the social factors which are so important in the up-building of Indian nationality. The Viceroy, immersed in files, "cases," and interviews with secretaries, is locked up in the summer at Simla, and is still more pressed by administrative duties in the legislative season at Delhi. A non-political Royal Viceroy would be free to travel more frequently, to visit seaside and other resorts, to set the tone of Indian and not merely high official society, and to generally encourage the development of social life in the provinces.

While the princely courts, as previously indicated, would promote art and literature in the widest form, so on an Imperial basis, the Viceroy would be the patron of all that is best in the representation of our emotional life. The two Tagores—the poet and the painter—have shown to Europe what India is capable of, even in these terrible days when everything outside politics is perforce neglected by the State. The Royal Court of Delhi and Simla would be the natural centre for encouragement of the arts. Indian music, both vocal and instrumental, operas, and tragedies appealing to the Indian temperament, would receive the encouragement which, as German history proves, helps to develop national talent and genius in such directions. In a word the Royal Viceroy, as I wrote in the article previously mentioned, "would put himself at the head of all movements, social, literary, economic and artistic, that improved the relations of all sections of society, that destroyed racial and religious particularisms, that helped to amalgamate the parts into a healthy whole."[1]

[1] *National Review*, February, 1907.

CHAPTER VIII

LOCAL SELF-GOVERNMENT

FROM the central authorities and the Viceroyalty in India, we may turn to a consideration of the local units in the work of public administration, for the connection between base and apex is more intimate than might be supposed by the superficial observer. Sir Charles Dilke once told me that Lord Ripon's local self-government policy in India was consciously influenced by the example of Alexander II in reorganising the *mirs*, the *volosts*, and the *zemstvos*. Whether this was the case or not, a bird's-eye survey of the Russian experience is pertinent to our study.

After the disastrous Crimean War, there was a great movement amongst the Court and the upper classes toward what they called "Europeanism." In his early years Alexander II strongly desired the introduction of at least the limited forms of representative administration which had served his Western neighbour so well. But *Festina lente* is ever the motto of despotism when its advance towards popular national government is voluntary. So the usual argument, which we in India have heard *ad nauseam*, of learning parish and county administration before attempting to participate in State affairs prevailed, and the local elective bodies, so well known to students of modern Russia for their constant clash with the bureaucracy and its autocratic principles, came into being. Owing to causes which it is beyond the scope of the present argument to examine, Alexander II and his son and grandson maintained a bureaucracy and left local self-government nominally to popular assemblies. The result for a period of nearly two generations was unhappy: constant interference, difficulties and conflict, sometimes leading to local revolution followed by merciless suppression. Such is the painful story of this famous experiment of nominally free local bodies existing side by side with an irresponsible central Government.

In no other part of the world, except nominally in India, has a Government founded on bureaucracy attempted to leave local affairs to popular assemblies. And in India Lord Ripon's reform, happily for all concerned, led to the bureaucracy retaining real power in local government, while leaving a nominal share to so-called representatives of the people in municipal and district boards. With the exception of the Bombay Municipal Corporation, and in somewhat less degree those of the two other Presidency cities, there is scarcely a civic authority in India that has had powers equal to those of the Russian local councils. And even in these three exceptional cases the executive work of the municipality, as well as a large amount of supervision, still remains in the hands of official chairmen appointed by the local Governments. Happily the constant friction arising from the Russian experiment has not been reproduced in India, for the good and simple reason that the real power has never been out of the hands of the bureaucracy.

It must not be inferred that the Civil Service can be charged with the conscious and preconceived ambition of throttling the local authorities. But in the political structure there are contradictory principles which cannot be simultaneously applied. An irresponsible bureaucracy depending for its power and promotion on a hierarchy of its own cannot work satisfactorily with really popular powers of municipal administration. The inadequacy of a common meeting ground makes friction inevitable. On the other hand, when there is a popular assembly in the capital associated with the Government, the relations of the district officials and the local bodies inevitably take on the character of co-operation. The natural dependence of both sides on central authorities gives each the consciousness that it is but an extension, in another form, of the power of the other.

Turning to the examples of some of the politically advanced countries, we find that invariably the responsibility of Government to the people has preceded the application of democracy to municipal rule. In England and Wales the power of Parliament, and especially of the House of Commons, was established for generations before local affairs were taken out of the hands of small and close corporations, such as parish vestries and magisterial benches. In other words the principle of popular control was applied first to the State as a whole, and subsequently to its component parts and local areas. The process was carried forward step by step after the Reform Act of 1832. It is important to note, however, that it was not consummated until after household franchise had been given, first to the boroughs in 1867, and finally to the counties in 1885. County councils, covering and co-ordinating both urban and rural self-government, were established by the Act of 1888, and six years later the Parish Councils Act set up popular assemblies in the smallest units of local government. It should be noted in passing that an English rural parish frequently comprises several hamlets each containing as many inhabitants as the ordinary Indian village.

It is true that in Japan local self-government preceded the establishment of the Diet in the Nine Years' Programme of 1881. But the real act of civic emancipation took place many years earlier. The political foundations of the Empire were modernised with the advent of the Mikado to Tokyo, and it was from the completion of the successes of the Imperialists over the Shogun and conservative elements that Japan's political rebirth dated. Similarly in Prussia, the real awakening of modernism took place long before the revolution of 1848 led to the introduction of a limited form of constitutionalism. The administration of Frederick the Great and, indeed, going back to the time of the Great Elector, though autocratic was yet national and impersonal, and so came nearer to modern ideals than the reader might suppose from a mere formal study of the Prussian Constitution.

In France, as all men know, the great Revolution was an attempt to gain control over the central administration. And in the long period from 1815 to 1870, we do not find the establishment of widely popular local assemblies proposed by anyone of the several régimes. It was not until the Third Republic came into being that, throughout the length and breadth of the land, including the smallest communes, the people took the helm.

Further historical examples are not required to emphasise the obvious conclusion. This is that in India an attempt to extend municipal autonomy widely without providing for each province-state the foundation of a really popular assembly directly representing every class and creed, with hundreds of thousands of electors behind it, would be inept, and might lead to something like a repetition of the long and sad record of the conflict of the central and local authorities in Russia. The lesson of history is that satisfactory reformation of subordinate authorities on a popular basis can only be carried out by a Government which is itself brought into touch, by an elective assembly, with the general consensus of reasonable opinion amongst the governed. Besides, to be really successful our local administration, like other political institutions, must be related to the surrounding conditions of development. It would be atrophied by merely mechanical imitation of other models or by doctrinaire attempts at uniformity. Even so important a step as the exercise of a wide discretion in local rating cannot be granted or refused on merely *a priori* grounds.

These being the ruling principles, I advocate the formation in each province-state of a ministry in the Cabinet relating to municipal and district authorities, and with powers similar to those of the Local Government Board in Whitehall, though modified in conformity with Indian conditions. Each provincial member of the federation would thus have a minister, in touch with its Cabinet and popular assembly, dealing with all the subordinate bodies. Thus, at last, real and general effect would be given to the principle laid down by Lord Ripon's Government that State control "should be exercised from without rather than from within," and that "Government should revise and check the acts of local bodies, but not dictate them."

While the powers of the new department would be similar in each province, in practice they would vary according not only to the conditions of the province-state itself, but of each district within the state. In this way the structure of local autonomy could be built up from the municipalities of the great towns down to the smallest village *panchayat*, and even the latter would differ according to the varying conditions of village life, and the standard reached by their respective communities. It is an idle dream to think that in the India of to-day, with its 37,000 miles of railways, with its posts, telegraphs and telephones, with its coming general use of motor traction, we can establish village communities such as were in existence in the pre-Mahomedan era. An economically self-contained and entirely independently administered village community as the general rule would be utterly unsuited for the expanding life of modern India. An attempt to restore such conditions would be like stopping the circulation of the blood to any of the various members of the human body. The principle of cohesion from the smallest up to the largest municipal unit, so successfully applied in England and Wales, must be followed. The Local Government Board, in every case where the village had a community sufficient to justify the procedure, would constitute an assembly of five, and the villagers would be linked up in groups to *tehsil* and district boards, and, when suburban, to municipalities. The larger authorities would be as free from official control as possible.

It will be seen that such a system would be essentially elastic, differing according to local conditions, in each province. Its progress and efficiency would be safeguarded, on the one hand by the Governor and Cabinet, assisted by the bureaucracy, and on the other hand by the popular assembly elected, not as now by a few English-speaking and well-to-do individuals, such as landlords and members of municipalities, but by thousands of every class, creed, and colour.

CHAPTER IX

THE CIVIL SERVICE

FROM the working of district and municipal bodies, we may turn to the great service which at present "guides and controls"[1] them. The administration of India as now constituted depends more on the Civil Service than on any other factor. In Britain and France the man in the street is the final support of the administration; in Germany the Government relies on the general consensus of opinion among the military, landed, and educated classes; and in Russia, under Tsardom, the army and the police were the final supports of autocracy. In India without the Civil Service government could not be carried on for any length of time.

But the bureaucracy is divided into two unequal portions. The first while numerically small, in importance and powers is far greater than the second. Recruited by competitive examination in London, it mainly consists of Englishmen, with a small percentage of Indians whose education has been completed in Britain. The second category, known as the provincial civil service, consists of large numbers recruited in India "to do the bulk of the ordinary executive and judicial work of the

[1] *Report of the Royal Commission on the Public Services in India*, Vol. I, p. 161.

districts and to fill the minor charges."[1] Adapting its character and qualities to those of the first group, this has been an admirable organism for carrying out the orders of what was formerly known as the "Covenanted Service." Without such direction and lead this element in the machinery would not be strong enough to execute the business of Government. In the same way as it has taken its colour from the *corps d'élite*, it will, should that service considerably change its character, adapt itself to the new circumstances. No outstanding reform can be effected by changing the conditions in this lower category. So the needs of the India of to-morrow compel us to concentrate our attention on the superior branch, leaving to the natural influence it exerts the bringing of the subordinate branch into line with the altered conditions.

The Indian Civil Service is one of the most extraordinary, interesting and distinguished corps in history. British India is essentially the result of its labours. To the question whether it has been a success or a failure a sincere, decided and unqualified answer cannot be given. It has succeeded absolutely and beyond any reasonable expectation in certain important grooves of national life ; yet, judging by results, it has also been a failure in some other important directions. It has succeeded in the activities that have been natural departments for a bureaucracy to deal with. It has failed when it has attempted to do work which, in a constitutionally governed State, falls to the monarchy, to the legislature, and to the nation.

The maintenance of law and order, the impartial

[1] *Report of the Royal Commission on the Public Services in India*, Vol. I, p. 161.

execution of ordinances, the gathering of taxes, the transparent honesty of finance, and the general freedom from the slightest taint of corruption have been beyond praise. The hundred and one sources of friction between the interests of the State and those of the individual have usually been adjusted with fairness and equity. Care has been taken in administration not to allow the interests of the poor and ignorant to be sacrificed to the cupidity of the rich, though elaborate codes passed by the legislatures have encouraged impoverishing litigation. Crime has been reduced to as low a limit as the poverty and ignorance of the people make possible, and the executive has always done its best to bring before the judicial tribunals (themselves largely composed of civilians) the real culprits. Material improvements, such as extended communications and the irrigation of tracts liable to scarcity, have been earnestly and consistently supported. In all these spheres, the smoothness of working and the general efficiency and success of the administration have been greater than in some European countries.

But none will deny that we have much further to travel in transforming unhappy features of life so common in Eastern lands. The grinding poverty of the masses, the recurring famines when rainfall is deficient or ill distributed, the ignorance and low standard of health general throughout the land, the absurd smallness of the income of the nation per head of population, and its natural result, a revenue far too small for the legitimate requirements of an immense Empire[1]—all these factors

[1] Exclusive of land revenue (which is not properly taxation) the average taxation per head, even on the incorrect assumption that all customs

lead to the conclusion that if India is to take her proper place, both within the British Empire and in contributing her quota to the stock of human progress, reform is inevitable. The narrow service by which she has been governed for over a century must, in the work of direction though not that of execution, be replaced by legislative and popular institutions such as have been successfully evolved in so many modern monarchies. The very constitution of a bureaucratic service bars it from directing those great national energies that a constitutional monarchy, in co-operation with the taxpayers, can mould to worthy ends. The direction and leading of the people, as well as the political education of the masses, now far too long overdue, must come in each of the province-states from the monarchy as represented by the Governor, and the people themselves through their representative institutions. Only by becoming conscious citizens do men make the greater sacrifices required for national advancement. A sullen and politically soulless people is peculiarly liable to sink into still greater poverty and ignorance.

In the legitimate and executive sphere of the work of the service, the necessity for considerable changes has long been apparent. The Royal Commission over which Lord Islington presided a few years ago was mainly designed to find ways and means for a larger admixture of Indians in the higher services. If its proposals to this end are adopted, they will not remove the fundamental objections to the existing dominance of the I.C.S.

and other duties are paid by inhabitants of British India, was only 2s. 1·1d. at the outbreak of war, according to the Statistical Abstract of British India, Fiftieth Number, 1917.

No Indian will deny that in an average district there is a certain atmosphere of aloofness between the collector and the people that cannot be other than unwholesome. After all, an Indian district magistrate is approximately in the position of a Russian governor during the Tsardom, or some of the provincial presidents in Germany and prefects in France. Yet how much more intimate in any European country are the general and business relations—apart from social contact—between the district administrator and the inhabitants than in India. It is a disadvantage, in this connection, that in Britain herself (owing to the wide diffusion of unpaid civic work) there are no similar authorities ; for had such a system existed in the United Kingdom, it would have afforded scope for more national practice in this class of work.

A method of bringing the service and the people into closer touch which has been widely advocated in India for years past has been that of simultaneous, or at least similar, examinations in India and in England, with a view to a large increase in the Indian element.[1] I have advocated this measure in the past, but fuller reflection has forced me to the conclusion that the mere addition of Indians will not solve the problem of aloofness between rulers and ruled. The Civil Service is an old and famous corporation that has done an immense work. As always, the doing of the work has given rise to a tradition. An *esprit de corps* has been developed with the consequence that the mere

[1] While rejecting the expedient, Lord Islington's Commission recommended a limited degree of direct recruitment in India, followed by three years' probationary study at English Universities contemporaneously with successful competitors, English and Indian, at the London examination to be taken at the school-leaving age.

increase of the Indian proportion will not render the service less distant from free contact with the people. It is not to be concluded that I deprecate *esprit de corps,* or criticise it in itself; but it is easy to have too much of a good thing. When the whole length and breadth of the country is divided into relatively small areas known as districts, and each district is vertically divided in charge of a governing few in the two branches of the service, with their *esprit de corps,* each member ruling many thousands, an unwholesome artificiality of life is inevitable.

The best corrective is to be found in a widened basis for public service. While retaining the I.C.S. on the lines of the present constitution, subject to changes such as were recommended by Lord Islington's Commission to greatly increase the Indian proportion of membership, we should bring district administration into closer touch with the people by non-official dilution. This may sound a very bold step, but it has been successfully tried in such European countries as have had bureaucratic administration. In Tsarist Russia, in Germany, in France, leading local gentlemen, whether members of the landed nobility or distinguished for their wealth, position, intelligence or honorary public services, have been often appointed governors, presidents, or prefects. After all, there is nothing in the work of an average Indian collector of so technical and difficult a nature as to render essential the very high educational tests which now keep men under preparation at the universities, or under probation in England, until they are midway through the third decade of life. The navigating officer or the civil engineer requires much more technical training than the Indian district officer. The present unavoidable restriction of European recruitment to very narrow limits has led to many posts hitherto filled by the higher branch of the Service being occupied by members of the subordinate branch, who have had a much less extensive and wholly Indian education. In the British appointments to be made by nomination, under the temporary Act of 1915, the educational standard will of necessity be lower than that normally exacted at the open examination, since the selections will be mainly of men who were prevented by war service from undergoing a university course. This inevitable breach in a tradition of sixty years might be extended advantageously to a utilisation of non-official agency. From amongst the ordinary citizens of India it would be possible to select many excellent district collectors for a term of years. A leading landlord, a public-spirited millionaire, or a lawyer or a gentleman at large who has given much of his time to local public service, might well be nominated to the headship of his district.

Such a dilution of the exclusively bureaucratic and professional element by local gentry and men drawn from the various categories of civil life would not only help to bridge the present lines of separation between rulers and the ruled. It would also give freshness and variety of outlook in the working of a machine which has become, to use the terms of Mr. Montagu's historic speech, "too wooden, too iron, too inelastic," not only at headquarters, but also in the districts. Even the professional administrator may find inspiration from the freshness of view of a neighbouring collector whose training and career have been on lines different to his own. The service tradition unduly tends to mould its members into the same type; and there is need for a widened range of selection for the higher posts to meet the complaints of rigidity, aloofness and over-professionalism. Moreover the "amateur" will be safeguarded against mistakes by the fulness and exactitude of the many Indian codes and regulations and the traditional watchfulness of the provincial secretariat.

The new element need not be limited to the Indian subjects of the King-Emperor. There is no reason why, say, a leading British merchant or publicist who has spent twenty years in, and learnt to love, Bombay or Madras, Calcutta or Karachi, should not be appointed to the charge of a district before he retires. Some people may smile at the idea of keeping in the country an Englishman, who has already "made his pile" in commerce, by the offer of four or five years of not overpaid public service. But I am confident that there are not wanting non-official Englishmen in the country —many names come readily to mind—who would gladly respond to the call to this new labour of love. Another, though smaller, field for such recruitment is to be found among the missionaries, some of whom, especially those engaged in higher education, may be prepared to serve India, the land to which they have devoted their lives, in a wider if secular sphere.

In the main, however, the non-official agency would be indigenous. There are many prominent Indians who would welcome the opportunity of such district service. That great nobleman the Maharaja of Darbangha, the first Indian member of the Behar and Orissa Executive Council, told me while holding the office that he regretted not being called to the more restricted, but in many ways not less helpful, position of a collector, in which he could see especially the opportunity of setting an example to others. While I have been writing this book, an Indian friend has been offered membership of one of the provincial executives. For various personal reasons, he regretfully declined the offer. I asked him whether if he had been offered the collectorship of his own beloved and beautiful native district, he would have made the great sacrifices involved in any acceptance of Government service. After serious reflection his answer was a decided " Yes."

The district collectors represent the Government to the people, and are the natural arms of the central authority. In the provinces of the future, on the lines advocated in these pages, I fail to see the need of those expensive go-betweens, the divisional commissioners. In the Madras Presidency there is no local officer above the head of the district, and I do not think the administration has suffered in consequence. Under the new system one or more members of the provincial Cabinet would carry on the work now devolving on the Board of Revenue. Whatever may have been the needs of the past the utility of maintaining in each province, other than Madras, several highly paid officials in charge of divisions would disappear.

CHAPTER X

THE POLICE

THE principle of a widened basis advocated in the preceding chapter for the I.C.S. should be applied *mutatis mutandis* to the police force, both on grounds of efficiency and for raising this service in public estimation. Under present conditions there is not mere aloofness, as in the Civil Service, but mistrust and even hostility on the part of vocal public opinion toward this necessary adjunct of government. No institution in the country is more abused than the police, and especially the division known as the Criminal Investigation Department. To listen to some popular politicians, one might suppose it to be an Okhrana reproduced on Asiatic soil with all the vices, though in milder form, of its notorious European prototype. Its leading members are sometimes described as *agents provocateurs*, and, to justify their own existence, held to be capable of such crimes as Azef and other Russian officials are known to have committed. When the perpetrator of an outrage or attempted outrage, such as the bomb-throwing at Lord and Lady Minto on their visit to Ahmadabad, disappears and is never traced, rumour attributes the crime to the dark forces of the police. In Calcutta one is repeatedly told by Bengali gentlemen of undoubted honour that the dividing line between the revolutionary bomb-throwers and the agents of the police is never distinct. Whenever a prominent man is run down by the Government and, either under the old Regulation of 1818 or by virtue of the Indian "Dora," segregated from his fellow-citizens, the average educated Indian attributes the internment to nothing but the machinations of the C.I.D.

Then, apart from politicians, thoroughly respectable middle-class citizens constantly talk and think of the police in a manner that is saddening and yet somewhat grotesque. In England only amongst the lowest classes of rough professional bullies and prize-fighters is the police referred to in the spirit in which it is regarded by the most respectable portions of the Indian *bourgeoisie.* It is true, as Fitzjames Stephen wrote many years ago, the difference in conditions makes the police more important and relatively far more powerful in India than in England. But that is not in itself a reason why they should be accused, as a body, of avarice, of corruption, of indifference to the real interests of the Government, and of only being anxious to fish in troubled waters. The official answer to such criticisms is that improvements are being steadily made, and that the fear inspired by the department is a remnant of the traditions of vanished native dynasties, when the absence of regularly enforced laws and of an independent Bench left the people at the mercy of the subordinate authorities. While it is acknowledged that the standards need to be raised, the average English official will tell the enquirer that the charges constantly brought against the police are most frequently attributable to fevered imaginations, and sometimes to bad consciences.

The fair-minded observer cannot accept without great qualification the very uncomplimentary popular version of the character of the police. Except for the higher positions it is Indian in composition. Substantial reforms were effected a dozen years ago as a result of the enquiries of the Police Commission. The members of the C.I.D. are almost all of them Indians, often good fathers of families, and though they are not recruited from the better ranks of society they usually come of respectable and conservative parentage. They are badly paid, and the general prospects of advancement are so poor that the wonder is that bribery and corruption are not more common. For after all, when one searches for the proofs of their dishonesty they are rarely to be found. The average Indian C.I.D. officer is poor throughout his life, and, retiring on a slender pension, he rarely leaves anything more than an average clerk usually possesses. Nor is it to be forgotten that in recent years in Bengal many such officers have been the victims of assassination as a result of their courage and resource in tracking down anarchical revolutionaries. It is unfortunate that there are not sufficient gentlemen and men of education in the police to give the people confidence in its working. There is great need for the police to be better paid and recruited from a higher stratum of society.

But in itself this would not be sufficient. Every government, and especially one like that of India where the highest personnel is mainly foreign, needs knowledge of the thought and conscious movements of the population. In irresponsible bureaucracies, whether inefficient, as were those of Turkey under Abdul Hamid and of Tsarist Russia, or well organised, like the rule of Britain in India, the Government is, for information, necessarily dependent on police reports. Notoriously this is particularly the case in Bengal, where the Permanent Settlement operates against contact of the Indian Civilian with the cultivating classes to the same degree as in *ryotwari* areas. But in all parts of the country the service whose natural sphere is to prevent and investigate crime takes the place, as a link between the Government and the people, which is filled under modern systems by popular representation. The only effective remedy is to establish elective legislatures, not, like the present travesties of representation in India, limited to a handful of people educated in English or rich, but on a wide basis, and directly drawn from every class, caste and community. Then, indeed, the voice of the people would be heard directly and distinctly. If ambitious members of the police force tried to influence policy by their secret reports, the prestige and self-reliance of an assembly directly elected by the people would prevail. The police would concentrate on their legitimate work and not be, as at present, an obscure and irresponsible factor in the inner councils of the realm.

Side by side with this external remedy for the present unhappy schism in the body politic, it is necessary to make the police more truly national. This need was recognised in the detailed recommendations of the Islington Commission, though it was held that a preponderating proportion of the superior officers, as in the case of the I.C.S., should be recruited in England. But all are agreed that a very substantial share of the highest posts now occupied by Englishmen should be filled by educated Indians. And as in the preceding chapter it was held that here and there ordinary citizens should be appointed district collectors in order to bring to the work of executive administration a fresh and less stereotyped angle of vision, so, in the police, important superintendentships should be filled in the same way. There is nothing in the duties of the average superintendent of so technical a nature as to make it necessary that the police administration in every city and district of the vast peninsula should be in purely professional hands.

Such a system would have a twofold advantage : it would be calculated to modify and possibly to remove the exaggerated but general mistrust of the police to which I have referred ; and it would give the professional heads the advantage of considering many things from the point of view of the non-professional citizen. As in the case of the I.C.S., unofficial Englishmen residing in the country should also be included in the range of selection. In Great Britain, in Germany, in France, and in Russia, various categories of citizens have been made use of for the higher police administration. It is not enough that a few members of the I.C.S., itself a close corporation, should be appointed to important positions, such as the inspector-generalships, as was recommended by the Police Commission in 1905. The principle of general co-operation in the detailed work of the administration between the professional servant of the State and the citizen must be followed in this department as well as in the headship of districts. These are the means for effecting, in relation to the protection of the life and property of the citizen from crime, that comprehension and mutual understanding between the non-official and the official which, in the most advanced states, has contributed so materially to the making of a united nation.

CHAPTER XI

THE JUDICIARY

HAPPILY the mistrust and dissatisfaction with which the police are regarded in India does not extend to the judicial system. On the contrary the application of British principles of legal justice is warmly cherished by the people. Some would say that it has contributed greatly to British "prestige." Yet in Indian society, where my somewhat peculiar position has brought me into contact with all sorts and conditions of men from princes to peasants, I have never heard the term used by my countrymen. Indeed, I have not found in any Indian language a true equivalent of this English word. Those usually given in dictionaries certainly raise quite different conceptions in the Oriental mind from that for which "prestige" stands to the Englishman. *Izzat* and *aatibar* are anything but synonymous therewith. The real equivalent for this word, as it is fondly used by some people, would be a high-handed disregard of right, justice, and even honour, in order to maintain the supremacy of the white man.

Happily for Britain, her rule in India is not generally associated with this aggressive form of Nietzschean supermanism, which flourishes vigorously only in its German home. Long before the military strength, the material improvements, or the other tangible activities of British rule are referred to by the average Indian, you may be quite sure that he will speak of its justice. To all classes in India, other perhaps than the ruling princes and their subjects, this is the essential quality needed for British rule in India. It is generally interpreted in the narrow sense of the relations between man and man, rather than the general expectation of fair play from the State and society at large towards the individual. But this second and wider conception is already gaining ground. There are many not usually associated with political activities, who reflect upon, and ask questions as to the ultimate right and mission of Britain in the country. The answer is to be found, in my humble judgment, in the co-operative federal constitution advocated in these pages. But even in the narrow sense of the relations of man to man and his business contact with the State, justice plays a predominant part in the political conception of the average informed Indian.

The general testimony is that the administration of justice is good and on the whole fair, but excessively long and costly. This is partly due to inherent causes, such as the wide range of variety in customs and usages among the various communities and in different parts of the country. Not only is the indigenous law of India personal, and divisible with reference to the two greatly preponderating elements in the population, Hindu and Moslem; but there is also a great body of recognised customary law, varying with the locality. Moreover, owing to the influence of Western jurisprudence, to the great body of case-law emanating from courts moulded on English models, to the advance of enlightened ideas, and to the progress of education, the ancient personal law of Hindu and Mahomedan has been subjected to modification and alteration in many important particulars. All this gives the overcrowded legal profession opportunity for prolonged and subtle disputation in almost every conceivable case relating to Indian social life. The codification of laws and of judicial procedure in India, originated by Macaulay, has been carried much further than in any other part of the British dominions. Though usually clear in wording, these codes are elaborate. While the opportunities for appeal are manifold gazetted public holidays are very numerous, owing to the necessity for observing the sacred days of the various communities. Nor are climatic and general conditions favourable to the obtainment of speedy decisions.

Obviously the expenditure of time and money involved by the slow pace of justice gives an advantage to the rich. In the case of the poor it is calculated to lead to certain loss, or perhaps a worse alternative, the sale of his rights to legal speculators. In the great towns either sharks or gamblers are ready to exploit every conceivable occasion for litigation, often ruining respectable families. In some instances the claims of litigants carried step by step to the Privy Council in London have remained unsettled for twelve or fifteen years. The scandal of these delays has been the subject of severe criticism, especially in the last year or two, in pronouncements of the Judicial Committee; and definite proposals have been made to the authorities in India to provide remedies by changes in the rules relating to appeals.

In the absence of any central appellate court in India "the right of access to the King in Council is eagerly cherished, and nothing must be done to infringe it, whether theoretically or actually, in the least degree."[1] Though it is obvious "that the avoidance of years of costly delay will operate in favour of even-handed justice as between all classes of His Majesty's Indian subjects,"[2] there is a strongly rooted belief in India that complete equity is bound up with the costly and time-exhausting formalities which have developed with the application of British jurisprudence. A case begun in the court of a subordinate judge in the *mofussil*, carried to the district judge, reviewed by the appellate side of the provincial High Court, and finally disposed of by the Privy Council in London, is regarded by the general public as issuing in a fair settlement of the disputes involved. But by the time the process of appeal is exhausted the property which has been the subject of contention has probably become no more than a fragment of its original value, when the cost of the proceedings is brought into account.

A curious but widespread idea amongst the British in India is that while the executive should continue to be overwhelmingly European, the judicial services can well be handed over to Indian management. For my part I have never been able to see the reasonableness of this marked differentiation. When all is said, Englishmen are in official positions in India because, after her chequered and tragic history, she is not able to satisfactorily settle her own affairs without the

[1] *The Times* in an article on the subject, 2 January, 1917.

[2] *Ibid.*

co-operation of people from happier lands. But this justification for British agency carries the necessary corollary that in all the main fields of State activity we need, for the present, the co-operation of both elements. If the executive is to be a close preserve for one race, then the other will lack opportunities for exercising what the history of the past, under an Akbar or a Shah Jehan, has proved to be the natural aptitude of the cultured Indian for executive functions. If the judiciary becomes the preserve of the Asiatic, then in what is morally the most important duty of the Government there is the assumption that British example and co-operation are no longer required. Those who argue thus overlook the consideration eloquently expressed by the distinguished first and only Indian to be called to the Judicial Committee of the Privy Council that "the equal administration of justice is the greatest glory of British rule in India, and furnishes the strongest claim to the loyalty of the people." Not only in the High Courts, but also in the districts, a fair admixture of the two races in high judicial office will for a long time to come produce the best results.

Yet here I must register a protest against one of the outstanding examples of racial injustice in India to-day, namely, that a Chief Justiceship has never been granted permanently to an Indian. There are Indian jurists well fitted to preside over provincial High Courts, and their exclusion on merely racial grounds must not be continued. Selection must be on the basis of merit alone. By all means let us have English Chief Justices in some of the provinces, but when there is an Indian on the Bench worthy of the highest position, it is absolutely unjustifiable to close the door of promotion because he is an Indian. Again, when an eminent jurist like Syed Ameer Ali is debarred from adding to his present functions on the Privy Council the judicial duties of a Law Lord appertaining to most of his colleagues, it is natural that his countrymen should resent such differentiation, knowing full well that he would be, on every ground, an ornament of the Upper House.

The federal system for India, advocated in these pages, carries the necessary implication of a Supreme Court for the whole peninsula, thus obviating, save in exceptional cases, the enormous cost in time and money of carrying the final appeal to London. An Indian Judicial Privy Council might well be formed, nor need its members be necessarily debarred from seats on the provincial Benches. Of course India must have a place in any scheme that may be adopted for conserving the unity of final appellate power within the Empire in London. Under such an arrangement two or three Indians should belong to the reconstituted Imperial Privy Council, and their *doyen* should be advanced to the peerage.

The need for replacing the present complicated and in some respects inequitable system of the admission of advocates and pleaders by a sensible and uniform plan is widely recognised. It is well known that the tests exacted for qualifying in India as an advocate of the High Court are much more severe than those imposed for calls to the Bar in England, and involve long and elaborate courses of study. Some of the conditions of admission of overseas students to the Inns of Court in London and Edinburgh have had the result of diverting young Indians to the Dublin law colleges. There is something ridiculous in the idea of a man called to the Bar in Ireland having privileges as a lawyer throughout India, with a hundred times greater population, denied to the graduates of the Indian law colleges. It is far from satisfactory that those who can afford to go abroad can claim higher privileges without the same studious efforts as are needed for the less affluent who remain in the country. Indeed, there are many cases of men entering for call to the Bar in Great Britain because they have found themselves unequal to the Indian tests. The manifold drawbacks of the system were well summarised in the valedictory report of Sir Charles Mallet as Secretary of the Indian Students Department. He pointed out that it is not uncommon to see a family which can ill afford the cost and perhaps hardly realises how heavy it will be, raise at some sacrifice the funds necessary to equip and maintain their boy studying for the Bar in England, "and then find all their labour wasted owing to the risks to which he has been exposed." I heartily support his suggestion that provision should be made for Indians to be called to the Bar in their own country and to secure in India the legal training they require.[1]

If an advocate system is preferred, a uniform standard for winning the right of advocacy should be established throughout the country. Englishmen wishing to practise at the Indian Bar should be expected to go through the Indian examination, in the same way as English doctors who contemplate setting up in France, or elsewhere

[1] *Report on the Work of the Indian Students' Department*, 1915-16. Cd. paper, 1916.

on the Continent, are required to pass the medical standards of the countries in which they settle. Since there is no language difficulty, it ought not to be a very formidable ordeal for a young Englishman, of good general education and legal knowledge, to pass the Indian advocacy examinations. The present system is a most haphazard and artificial growth; it is partial in its incidence, unduly favouring the well-to-do, and there is urgent need for its supersession by a more natural and sensible plan.

The changes suggested for both Bench and Bar would not in themselves be sufficient. Side by side with a splendid and honourable, but expensive, judiciary there is need for official encouragement of arbitration. The Sinn Feiners, as a sign of impatience with the Imperial connection, have urged the institution of non-official arbitration boards throughout Ireland, with a view to reducing the law courts to inactivity. A like idea has occasionally been heard from the lips of Indian extremists; but the existence of such anarchical motives in implacable quarters need not blind us to the considerable merit of the idea of arbitration boards side by side with judicial benches, and as alternatives to costly litigation. The people in India, no doubt, are as free to settle their disputes by mutual arbitration as those of other countries. But initiative and resource are not always conspicuous in human nature, particularly under tropical skies and when handicapped by illiteracy and poverty. The general freedom to choose arbitrators is not the same thing as having ready at hand men officially recognised as capable of exercising such quasi-judicial functions.

I strongly urge, therefore, the institution in every district and also in the great cities of regular panels of unpaid but willing men, with common sense and general honesty as arbitrators. Many gentlemen now on the roll as justices of the peace, and others willing to thus serve the community, would be nominated by the Governors as members of the boards for the various districts. The composition of the panels would be known, and while the courts would be prepared to leave to litigants an effective option, they should encourage resort to arbitration. The present privilege of private reference to arbitrators would not be curtailed; but, in addition, when cases not involving important questions of law went to the courts, the parties would receive from the judge a suggestion of submission to some of the arbitrators on his panel, as a welcome alternative to the expense and delay of regular litigation. The tendency would be toward avoidance of the costly processes of the law courts, except in cases of substantial importance, or of an abstruse nature. The panels would do much to mitigate the litigious tendencies which have so impoverishing an effect upon the cultivating classes.

CHAPTER XII

OVERSEAS SETTLEMENTS

HAVING considered the constitution of an Indian federation and the framework of civil and judicial administration by which it should be accompanied, we may widen our survey to discuss India's relations first with other portions of the Empire and next with foreign countries, before we deal with the problems of defence and internal economic and intellectual development. It is to be remembered that from before the dawn of Indian history the advent of conquerors by way of the Northern passes has been coincident with some degree of emigration, and at times this must have been on a considerable scale. At no time of which record exists has India been wholly isolated and self-contained in the matter of the movement of population.

Thus we have many evidences of a tendency in ancient days toward the spreading of Brahmanical culture beyond the confines of the peninsula. Indian legends, folk-lore, early epics and romances give abundant proofs, when all allowance is made for hyperbole and extravagant metaphor, of the immemorial struggle for expansion of the Aryan races in their contact with the dark aborigines carrying them across the seas. The great part the island of Ceylon, for example, plays in these semi-historic legends is well known to Western readers of the Ramayana. Indian influence and culture long dominated the Malay Peninsula and Archipelago, and went further eastwards. In the depth of Cambodia, one of the protectorates of Indo-China, are the immense and wonderful ruins of Angkor Wat and Angkor Thôm—miles of stately edifices covered with carvings of the most delicate and elaborate description, and retaining to a great extent their beauty and strength, although they are sunk in tropical forests, overgrown, deserted, and abandoned of man. Angkor Thôm is dated by experts before the Christian era, and the temples of Angkor Wat were certainly finished by the fifth or sixth century. Well-nigh every stone of them is carved, some with Hindu and some with Buddhist figures. To this day certain ceremonies performed in Cambodia resemble distantly the Brahmanical cult, while the Anamese religion is a vague and very tolerant Buddhism, which in practice resolves itself chiefly into the worship of ancestors.

The natural tendency toward external expansion on the part of the most advanced Indian races was checked from the third century of the Christian era by the hopeless disorganisation of Indian society, arising from such causes as the prolonged struggles between the Brahman hierarchy and the Buddhistic and Jain cults, and the economic effects of cycles of deficient rainfall in over-populated areas. India lost contact with her children beyond the seas, and left the Brahmanical influences in the Malay Archipelago to wither away, or at all events to be greatly modified by the habits and customs of the aboriginal peoples. Hence when Islam reached Java and other islands of the Archipelago some ten centuries later, it had little difficulty in succeeding to the dominant position formerly occupied by the Brahmans, and in establishing Moslem civilisation on durable foundations. Meanwhile Hindu society lost its cohesion and stability, and its expanding and colonising powers came to an end. From the sixth or seventh century down to the fourteenth or fifteenth century, though minor communications existed between India and the East and there was some interchange of commodities westwards, there was little attempt at regular settlement beyond the seas.

The early struggles of the Western European Powers for dominance of the Indian seas, after the discovery of the Cape route, had their reflex action in reviving Indian overseas enterprise. A tendency to expansion across the Indian Ocean to the African coast arose. It steadily grew, amid all the mutations of the ensuing centuries, until in Victorian times the Eastern littoral of the vast African continent became the principal outlet for the emigrating classes of the country. There also developed under British rule a stream of Indian emigration to the West Indies, Mauritius, and islands of the Pacific, such as Fiji. In the same way, a minor current in the early years of the present century turned the thoughts of emigrants to the Pacific coast of Canada and the United States. Still, apart from the easy access to, and return from, plantations in Ceylon and the Straits Settlements, the main trend was toward Africa. There were hopes amongst instructed Indians at least of the foundation on the other side of the Indian Ocean of a daughter country. But the vision was disturbed by the conflict of interests which led the white colonists to impose restrictions and disabilities upon the Indian communities.

The first cause for anxiety came when, in the southernmost part of Africa, in Natal and the two Dutch Republics, the severe pressure of anti-Asiatic legislation and executive action was widely felt. The grievances of the emigrants and settlers whose labour had been eagerly sought in the first instance for the agricultural and plantation development of Natal were taken to heart by their fellow countrymen at home. The marked impression made throughout India by the difficulties confronting the Indians in South Africa—difficulties which, after all was said and done, were not surprising in view of the disadvantages from which India herself suffered—can only be attributed to an instinctive consciousness that one of the dearest aspirations of the country, though scarcely formulated as yet, was in danger. India was groping her way, even then, to a more honoured and recognised place in Imperial partnership. Rich and poor, educated and ignorant, men of all races and creeds, conservatives like Sir Mancherjee Bhownaggree (who eloquently pleaded the cause of justice for his countrymen in Parliament), and those of advanced opinions and idealism, like Mr. Gandhi, the Indian leader in South Africa, were united and determined. In a very real sense a *cri du cœur* was raised by India for the protection of her absent children.

Behind the natural indignation and sorrow aroused by the knowledge of the indignities suffered lurked the almost unconscious fear of a great danger that was not adequately appreciated by the British people at the time. Long before the partition of the mainland dominions of the Sultan of Zanzibar amongst the European Powers, East Africa had been the principal field abroad for Indian activity in higher services than those of manual labour. The contribution the Indian has rendered to civilisation and material development in East Africa dating from before the advent of European influence in Zanzibar and on the adjacent mainland, can scarcely be over-estimated. Commerce in every branch, the development of agriculture, the supervision of works of public utility, the higher forms of skilled labour, the exercise of no insignificant share of political influence amongst the chieftains—all these were in Indian hands for many a decade before Europeans began the work of thorough and scientific exploration of the East African mainland. And the pioneers of this great enterprise, Stanley, Kirk and others, were indebted to Indians, such as the late Sir Tharia Topan, for the organisation of their expeditions into the interior. The value of Indian merchants and traders to this part of Africa was vastly increased by the establishment of British rule in the equatorial zone and through to Uganda. Indians not only constructed the railway from the coast to Lake Victoria Nyanza; they were the pioneers of the intercourse with the interior of which it is the chief link.[1]

During the closing years of the nineteenth century, however, it was discovered that the plateau

[1] "It is the Indian trader who, penetrating and maintaining himself in all sorts of places to which no white man could go, or in which no white man could earn a living, has more than anyone else developed the early beginnings of trade and opened up the first slender means of communication."—*My African Journey*, 1908, by the Right Hon. Winston Churchill, then Under-Secretary for the Colonies.

of British East Africa offered an excellent field for European colonisation. The resort thereto has not been very large, but has comprised farmers from Great Britain, and also some colonists from South Africa who had not succeeded there so fully as they had hoped. But the influence of the white settlers was very great, and the twentieth century was still in its infancy when it became evident that there existed in embryo most of the factors which had led to the troubles of the Indians in South Africa. In a country which, till then, India had had reason to regard as almost a daughter state, a relative handful of white settlers claimed the reservation to Europeans of the whole of the fertile highlands, covering an area from 25,000 to 30,000 square miles. The regulations passed under the influence of the white settlers exposed the Indian subjects of His Majesty to growing disabilities and restrictions.

Inevitably the feeling between the two sections became one of sullen, if usually unexpressed, hostility. Every year there was, on the one side, a sense of injustice and fear of repetition of the distressing experiences of fellow-countrymen in South Africa; while, on the other side, there were selfish claims and a dislike for the enterprise of people of dark colour looked upon as a conquered and inferior race even in their own country. The Indian settlers in East Africa were mostly of a more advanced and prosperous class than those which had gone to the Natal plantations under indenture, and some of them were men of wealth. Hence they were able to visit their native land much more frequently than South African Indians. They poured the tale of their sorrows into sympathetic ears. I do not lose a due sense of proportion when I say that one of the deeper causes, if not of discontent or disaffection, at any rate of the distrust of England and Englishmen that appeared on the surface in India in recent years was the strained relationship between Indians and their white fellow-subjects in East Africa. A rankling sense of injustice was aroused by the reservation of the best lands for Europeans, and by a succession of ordinances and regulations based on an assumption of race inferiority. It must be remembered that such a state of injured feeling evokes a subconscious spirit, which, in a few decades, may lead to results out of all proportion in importance to the original causes.

The situation was the more to be deplored since British East Africa had German territory as her colonial neighbour to the south, and there the relations of Indians with the administration were on a different basis. At first, in the eighties the Teutonic Government suspected the Indians of strong sympathies with the original Arab owners of the soil, and of carrying on an illicit trade in firearms with the Arabs and the natives. Consequently in shaping its original course German rule was hard and severe toward the Indians. In the early nineties, however, the Germans came to the sound conclusion that Indian assistance was requisite for the full commercial development of their colony. While, as the Indians often told me at the time, the Germans were hopelessly ignorant of Indian divisions, communities, castes, and internal organisation, they did make an effort to understand and tolerate them.

When the nineteenth century had almost run

its course a further Indiaphile movement took place. The German authorities not only encouraged Indian mercantile and skilled labour colonists, but dreamt of inducing Indian agriculturists to immigrate on a large scale on a basis of permanent land occupancy. When I was visiting my followers in German East Africa in the autumn of 1899, the Government of the colony made a number of definite propositions to me for some eight hundred Indian farmers of good class to settle there. The authorities were prepared to hand over to each settler a prospective farm much larger than anything he tilled in his native land, and to do so free of charge and with certain guaranteed privileges. From the Indian standpoint the idea was *prima facie* attractive, and I carried out some investigations as to how it might be put into execution with advantage to the cultivators.

When I visited Berlin in the autumn of 1900 to see what further progress could be made, an insuperable difficulty arose. With characteristic thoroughness the Wilhelmstrasse laid down the condition that the agriculturists to be selected should renounce their British allegiance and accept that of the German Emperor before entering on the enjoyment of the privileges they were to receive. Naturally, we were not prepared to agree to so many hundreds of Indians giving up their status as British subjects. I urged that no such difference should be made between the farmers and the Indians engaged in commercial pursuits in German East Africa.

It should be remembered that these negotiations were carried on when Germany was still regarded as the best friend of Britain in Europe, notwithstanding occasional aberrations on the part of her versatile ruler such as the telegram to Kruger in reference to the Jameson raid. Queen Victoria's long reign had not reached its conclusion, and the affection and intimacy of the two Courts were generally known, William II being a constant visitor to Osborne and Windsor. Russia was then looked upon as the arch-enemy of British security in the East. We had almost gone to war with France a short time earlier over the Fashoda incident; and the general British attitude in reference to the Dreyfus affair was like a burning sore dividing the two nations. Still, even under such favourable international conditions, I could not agree to a scheme which would have deprived a number of fellow-countrymen of British citizenship. I therefore dropped the project, cherishing the hope that before long the Germans would come to see that the demand was unreasonable, and that they would not allow it to stand in the way of the material benefits their colony would derive from the work and skill of Indian farmers.

The opening of the present century, however, was marked by a gradual and growing estrangement between England and Germany, which reached its zenith, short of war, with the visit of the Kaiser to Tangier. Inevitably the change reacted on the relations of Germans and Indians in East Africa. Up to a year or two before the dogs of war were loosed, there was a growing and general feeling of aversion between the Indians and the authorities of German East Africa. After the Balkan wars there was a distinct rapprochement between England and Germany, and Bethmann-Hollweg evidently hoped to separate England from Russia and France before the day came for attacking the two latter countries. This tendency had its echo in East Africa, and the German authorities began to talk of placing the Indians on the same commercial and political level as the Greek settlers. This new angle of vision was regarded with much satisfaction by the Indians. Then came the Great War, and of course a radical change in the situation, in which the Indians in the colony suffered severely at German hands.

CHAPTER XIII

INDIA'S CLAIM TO EAST AFRICA

THE preceding chapter has shown that amongst the many questions to which the war has given a new orientation and which cannot be left unsettled is that of healing the running sore of Indian resentment of the policy toward her sons of some other overseas portions of the Empire. It has to be recognised that there are some dominions, such as Canada and the temperate regions of South Africa and Australia, that have been won to civilisation by the white races, and are more congenial to their expansion, and where the view is taken that the structure of society should be predominatingly, and in some cases almost wholly, of Western type and composition. But no such claim can be made in regard to East Africa, whether British or hitherto German. These regions have provided a field for Indian immigration and enterprise from time immemorial, and we have seen that Indians played a conspicuous part in their development before the white man came on the scene as a settler.

In some British quarters in India an effort has been made, often by indirect methods, to lead public opinion to look upon Mesopotamia as the natural field for Indian expansion, and the inference has been that East Africa might be left to the white subjects of the King. With all due respect, my countrymen are not prepared to accept this change of venue. While every Indian patriot who has given thought to the matter aspires to drawing the peoples of the trans-Gulf territories to a freewill outer federation with the Indian Empire, he has no desire that India should impose herself on these already civilised and settled regions. To Mahomedans, from prince to peasant, there is something singularly abhorrent in the idea of an economic conquest at the expense of the Arab, and settlement in a spirit of expropriation on lands that are historically contiguous to the cradle of Islam. Nor can the Hindu desire to see some hundred thousands of his race lost in a Moslem country, far removed from the life and traditions of India, with the prospect that within two generations they would be absorbed in Islam.

Regarding the matter from the standpoint of economics, Mesopotamia under the new conditions will always be open to Indian trade, friendly non-colonising immigration and financial enterprise. In East Africa, on the other hand, if the Indian loses his association with the country, the probabilities are that he will be unable to return there, and can no more look across the Indian Ocean for a field of expansion than to Canada or Australia. Again, though Mesopotamia is a rich country potentially, yet, like Egypt and Sind, it is dependent for prosperity on water supply and irrigation, and the area of cultivation cannot be indefinitely extended. Under settled rule the Arab population will grow and prosper. In my judgment therefore not more than a relatively small number of Indians can profitably make the land of the Tigris and

Euphrates their settled home. Turning eastwards we find that Southern China and Siam, the Malay Archipelago and Peninsula, while legitimate and hopeful spheres for the development of trading relations with India, are far too overcrowded for any possibility of setting up Indian immigration, other than that which exists in the case of Malaya to help in the provision of an imported labour supply. The vast tracts of Northern Australia, though suitable for Indian industry and practically useless if manual labour there is to be confined to white races, are still too little known and too undeveloped for the purpose of Indian immigration, even if the way was not blocked by the racial policy of the Commonwealth.

The moral indignation of the Indian peoples which has wiped the indenture system off the slate has carried some publicists so far that their arguments amount to a demand for the virtual interdiction of labour emigration except to such near neighbours as Ceylon and the Straits Settlements. It is alleged that India herself needs all the labour at her command, that though her population is large and rapidly increasing, there are still sparsely peopled tracts where, by a system of "internal emigration," ample employment may be found for the surplus labour of the more densely populated areas.

This argument is economically short-sighted and politically separatist in effect if not in intention. At a time when India is claiming a new and more equal place in the comity of Empire, it would be unjust and reactionary to deprive the landless labourer of external opportunities to better his condition and prospects. It would mean forcing him to remain in a lower level of comfort than that provided elsewhere by his industry and thrift. To claim that all State intervention, in the shape of protection and regulation, should cease now that the indenture system has disappeared, would be to place great obstacles in the way of voluntary emigration, for in the present state of mass ignorance the would-be emigrant needs to have behind him the protecting care of Government. For these reasons I cannot range myself on the side of the vehement opponents of the scheme of assisted voluntary labour emigration and land settlement, with rights of repatriation if desired, drawn up by Lord Islington's inter-departmental committee in 1917 in respect to British Guiana, Trinidad, Jamaica, and Fiji, to supplement the existing thriving Indian colonies there. The scheme should have been worked out in India rather than at Whitehall, but this is an objection to procedure and not to the principles of the scheme. Not only does the opponent of any and every reasonable form of regulation lay himself open to the suspicion of desiring to keep wages low in India by blocking the way of any external competition; he also plays into the hands of white colonists in various lands who seek for their own purposes to keep out the thrifty and industrious Indian cultivator.

To the Indian conversant with public affairs there is something singularly revolting in the desire of a mere handful of his white fellow-subjects to keep East Africa as a preserve for themselves. There are but some 65,000,000 whites in the British Empire, and they have for their almost exclusive enterprise not only the United Kingdom (of which Ireland certainly needs population and colonisation as much as any country, at least in the temperate zone), but the immense tracts of Canada, Australia and South Africa proper. Yet a small section desires to bar to the 315,000,000 Indian subjects of the King the lands of East Africa, to which their labour and enterprise for centuries have given them an unanswerable claim.

That claim is strongly reinforced by consideration of Imperial duty to promote the interests of the country most directly concerned. It is peopled by vast numbers of dark and aboriginal tribes. India, too, has her Bhils and other wild tribes in much the same stage of development. Her immigrant sons must feel stronger sympathy and toleration for the Africans than the white settler, and will be singularly fitted to help to raise them in the scale of civilisation. The Indian cultivator and the Indian craftsman do some things as these children of the wilds do them, only they do them much better. Indians would teach the natives to plough, to weave, and to carpenter; the rough Indian tools are within the comprehension of the African mind, and even Indian housekeeping would be full of instructive lessons to the negro. He does not in fact learn from the European planters, because their methods are so far above his head; they belong to another world which has no suggestions for him. Somaliland offers an object lesson of what the African can gain from contact with a superior but kindred civilisation—in this case, of course, the Arab. I am gratified to know that this aspect of the matter strongly appeals to my good friend Sir Theodore Morison after careful observation and widespread travel in "German"

East Africa as a political officer attached to Belgian and other fighting units from the summer of 1916.

There is a further argument for East Africa as the most appropriate field for Indian colonisation and settlement. Nations and peoples instinctively gravitate toward certain lands, and yet, when we analyse this semi-conscious trend, we see that it is founded on reason. When East Africa becomes a real Indian colony, Indian commerce and enterprise will have outlet for a great trans-African development, with the Congo, Egypt, North and West Africa, and the South. The East Coast will be for India a shop window open to the West. If it is recognised that India has a special part to play in African civilisation and that she needs room for expansion westwards there, we must have clear guarantees that her sons are not to be persecuted out of these lands or artificially prevented from fully developing an immigration so beneficial to the country. Both British East Africa and what have hitherto been German territories ought to be transferred to India to be administered as a colony by the central Government. Administration would be carried on, to a great extent by British and Indian members of the I.C.S. It would be for India to put all her pride and patriotism into the development of these great regions. This would be her special contribution to post-war reconstruction, and by the measure of her success she would be largely judged. Indian men of science will be wanted to tackle the diseases of men and cattle; Indian geologists, foresters, and engineers to conserve or develop the country. The specialised professional schools at Pusa, Rurki, and Dehra Dun, and all the Indian universities must give of their best; and still the country would absorb more.

What would please India most and afford the best guarantee of progress, as already suggested, would be the transfer of the administration of German, as well as British, East Africa to the Government of India. Still, after four years of war, we must face facts squarely. Though disappointing, especially to those who have shared at heavy cost in conquering the German colony, it is at least conceivable that, in the interests of a general settlement, the country may be restored to Germany when the peace treaty is signed. American opinion will be an important factor, and President Wilson (who repeats, in this world war, the ideal rôle that Alexander I played a hundred years ago) has ranged himself and all for which he stands against aggressiveness on either side, so long as Prussian militarism is crushed. The Prime Minister has announced that the German colonies are "held at the disposal of a conference, whose decision must have primary regard to the wishes and interests of the native inhabitants of such colonies." Those interests in East Africa are unquestionably in the direction of a free field for India's civilising mission. Germany's natural sphere of expansion lies in the under-populated and largely Germanised Baltic provinces which have fallen to her, temporarily at least, by Russia's defection from the Allied cause.

Still, should the retrocession of German East Africa be decided upon, then British East Africa, including the island of Zanzibar, ought, in all fairness, to be transferred to the Government of

India. This course was recommended by Gokhale in his last political testament, written a few days before his death in February, 1915, and which it was my privilege to make public, in accordance with his death-bed directions, in the summer of 1917. It would be vastly better both for the Sultan of Zanzibar and his people that he should be an Indian prince dealing with the Government of India than that he should remain in existing relationships with the Foreign Office. There is no relevance in the argument that as the chief part of the work of conquering German East Africa fell to the South African forces, and not to the Indian Army, the Union has a first claim. This contention, which I have heard even from high British officials in India, I can only characterise as mean and un-English. India is without self-government; her military forces are entirely at the disposal of Whitehall; they are sent to the great and urgent danger point in the early weeks of the war, to help in saving Belgium and France and in saving England herself from the menace of German occupation of Calais; by the thousands her sons, facing the rigours of trench warfare in a northern winter, die in the fields of Flanders—and then this preoccupation and later calls to Mesopotamia, Palestine, and elsewhere are used as a ground for keeping Indians from their natural outlet across the Indian Ocean! The conclusion has only to be stated to be condemned by all "sane Imperialists."

German West Africa is both geographically and strategically the natural acquisition for the South African Union. This large addition to the already immense field of their unified territory should be amply sufficient to satisfy the aspirations of the sparsely sprinkled Anglo-Dutch races of the Southern hemisphere. German East Africa, if retained, and British East Africa clearly ought to belong as a colony to the Government of India, to be administered as the common heritage of the autonomous provinces and principalities under a federal system. These territories must be open to full and free Indian enterprise. It would be a strange outcome of the war, and a cynical recognition of Indian loyalty, if under the British flag the portion of East Africa where Indians prospered when it was in German hands should, together with British East Africa, be closed to the enterprise of Indian subjects of the King. The risk of such a political scandal, so harmful to Imperial solidarity, is by no means imaginary and remote, as was shown a few months ago by the exclusion of two Punjab barristers from Mombassa, in spite of the representations of the Government of India on their behalf to the British East African authorities. It is plain that when a colony gets into the hands of a few thousand white settlers, there is little chance of India obtaining fair play.

As to the problem of Indians in South Africa, Canada, and Australia a reasonable *modus vivendi* ought not to be difficult, having regard to the spirit of mutual comprehension which was shown by the Dominion and Indian delegates to the Imperial War Conference in 1917. The Indians permanently settled in any of those countries should be guaranteed the ordinary rights of citizenship. In the case of future Indian migration, clear distinctions ought to be made between travellers for instruction and pleasure, the commercial representatives of large Indian houses, and such Indians belonging to the liberal professions as desire to make their home in these countries, on the one hand; and on the other hand, the would-be emigrants who live on an economically lower standard than that of the white man in the labour and lower middle-class markets.

Under this policy India would have her own outlet for colonial expansion, and her well-to-do travellers, her commercial representatives, and her scientists and professional classes would secure a regular position in those British Dominions which not unnaturally are determined to maintain systems of protection against under-selling and under-serving the white labourer and the small trader. Such a solution should meet the legitimate rights and interests of both sides, and finally dissipate those strained relations between India and the Dominions concerned, which stand in the way of the growth of Imperial solidarity.

CHAPTER XIV

FOREIGN POLICY

PASSING from India's relations with other parts of the Empire to her foreign policy, we have to remember the two forms of intercourse between nations: one entirely commercial, economic, cultural, and amicable and not likely to be suspended by clash of political interests; the other comprising contact with neighbouring lands or with certain groups of governments, where purely political and military interests are liable to bring sudden collapse to the friendly flow and exchange of merchandise and ideas. To illustrate: the relations of Great Britain with Bolivia or Peru, Norway or Denmark are of such a nature as to make a conflict of arms a practical impossibility. But in respect to France, Germany, Russia, Japan, and indeed all the "Great Powers," there has always been the possibility of a serious clash of interests between her and one or more of them. India's position is complicated by her membership of the world-wide British Empire, whose immense interests are of importance to every component part. Thus India, in common with the self-governing Dominions, may find herself at war with countries with which she has few points of direct contact or friction. These wider problems of Empire, however, are outside the scope of this study, since their quiescence or settlement essentially depends on the United Kingdom. We are concerned here only with such issues as might possibly lead the British Empire into entanglement through India's vital interests.

It is obvious that these possibilities might arise in relation to Japan and China, to what has hitherto been Asiatic Russia, to Persia and Afghanistan, to Germany and Turkey. Siam and the Dutch and French Colonies are too weak to threaten serious complications in the future for India. China, which would have been India's most dangerous rival and neighbour had she been a military power or even a nation with a settled government, is divided by internal conflict, by want of political unity, and by general backwardness. In her helplessness she fears the aggression of others, and can have no thought of a "forward" policy of her own.

With Japan the case is entirely different, and though, happily, Britain and Japan are old allies and friends, yet India must always bear in mind the expansionist ideals of the Island Empire. No doubt Japan has proved herself to be essentially conservative and moderate, with a far-sighted policy, free from vanity and merely aggressive Jingoism. Nor has she sought the form of power without the reality. Her annexation of Korea and protectorate over Southern Manchuria have given her a free and dominating position in Eastern Asia. Now, with the collapse of Russia, and Japan's intervention at Vladivostok with Allied approval, Northern Manchuria and South-Eastern Siberia may be drawn within her orbit. We must not forget that, cooped up in her long and narrow islands and with a population rapidly approaching sixty millions, she is conscious of the need for exterior lands for exploitation and management. Will she be entirely satisfied with the possession of Northern China, and the general hegemony of trade and economic position over the rest of the Far East, or will she need expansion southwards ? This great problem of the future does not immediately concern our present study, for Japan must have acquired and consolidated a position over the French and Dutch Colonies before she is *vis-à-vis* with India. Yet no really conscientious Indian patriot can afford to ignore the power of the Rising Sun. In a later chapter I indicate the necessity for Indian naval and military preparation in case of need in the Bay of Bengal and the South-Western Pacific.

To the west India has two neighbours with whose true interests, happily, hers do not clash. Persia and Afghanistan have small and scattered populations ; but each, apart from their desert and mountain tracts, are ample enough in potentially good agricultural and manufacturing areas to be equal, the former to Germany and the latter to Italy. They could easily maintain far larger populations than now. Neither of them can ever be strong enough to menace India's position within the British Empire. On the other hand, it is to the manifest interest of India that these two neighbours should be under sane, orderly, and progressive autonomous rule.

Toward the South Asiatic Federation of to-morrow a truly independent Persia and Afghanistan would be drawn by every motive of self-interest.

Their climatic and economic conditions differ so widely from those of India that a natural outlet for exchange of commodities with their great southern neighbour would be ever a force moving them toward a good understanding. The need is for a policy that will first raise both countries to such a position of strength and independence as will remove from their governing classes all suspicion of being an object of mere desire of possession to their neighbours. Given such confidence, we may anticipate that Persia and Afghanistan would willingly enter a great and heterogeneous South Asiatic Federation, first through commercial and customs treaties, and secondly by such military conventions as would assure their position.

Something of the kind here foreseen has already been witnessed in embryo in Afghanistan, though it has not gone far yet either in developing Afghan independence and strength, or in bringing her into less meagre economic and cultural relations with India. The need is for an Afghanistan with a modern Army guaranteeing her safety from sudden attack from any quarter, and yet with railway communication through various doors, alike with India, with Persia, and with her northern neighbours. The same holds true of Persia, though there, alas! we have not seen the country being consolidated in our day under a man of genius, such as the late Ameer Abdur Rahman Khan. Still Persia, like Afghanistan, has great advantages over many other Asiatic peoples, in being a real nationality in the European sense of the word. That nationality has endured for long centuries, and has been in its time one of the leading factors in the history of the Old World The Afghans cannot look back to such inspiring traditions; but under the far-sighted rule of Dost Mahomed and Abdur Rahman Khan in the nineteenth century they exhibited a ready consolidation of national instincts. Thus we have two national states of large territory, but with small and scattered populations, on the most vulnerable part of India's great land frontiers.

In these circumstances the interests of the Empire and of India demand a clear and definite policy, and one that is happily simple, honourable, and moral. Our influence must be exerted to the full to make Persia and Afghanistan strong, independent national entities. And then we may be sure of receiving from them advances towards economic and military union on a free and equitable basis. The dismemberment of Russia at Brest-Litovsk releases us entirely from the moral and other disadvantages of the Anglo-Russian Convention of 1907—some of them powerfully catalogued by Lord Curzon in Parliament in the following year. However convenient the instrument may have proved for the time being it was not in keeping, to say the least, with the principles for which the British Empire has been pouring out blood and treasure in the last four years. Now that titanic forces have reduced the Convention to a dead letter we can resume the policy of the later Victorian times toward Persia, and win back the confidence of the people of that country. Not the least of the advantages of so doing will be that of strengthening our position in relation to some of the greater foreign dangers that lie ahead. I note with pleasure the revival of the Persia Society, under the presidency of Lord Lamington, to develop sympathy under the new conditions between Britain and Persia, and to encourage the study of questions of common interest.

Eastwards from Persia and Afghanistan there is an isolated State with approximately a similar position in relation to India. Tibet, however, from geographical and other causes is yet too backward to permit of our taking the same measures as toward these great kingdoms. But here too, on principle, we have a moral and beneficial policy to pursue. It is to leave the Tibetans to manage their own affairs as they think best, while encouraging such cultural and economic relations as should be satisfactory to both parties.

The vast upheavals of the war have entirely changed our outlook as to the greatest of Indian foreign problems, namely, the danger of aggression from some European Power or combination. From 1835 to 1905, a period of fully two generations, the fear of Russian advance southwards was like a nightmare to the rulers of India. To prepare for Muscovite attempts to invade India was the foundation of Anglo-Indian foreign policy for those seventy years. For the greater part of that time the people of India had not awakened to political life, and the general indifference to everything outside personal or caste interests was marked. But one international question even then reached the imagination of the poorest and most ignorant classes in India, and that was the possibility of a war with Russia. A vivid memory of my childhood is the immense impression which the Panjdeh incident in 1885 made on mill-hands in Bombay and gardeners in Poona. The two Afghan Wars had brought home to the humble peasant the problems of the North-West, and were regarded as striking preludes to the inevitable and mighty struggle between England and Russia in Asia. In one of his early books Lord Curzon foreshadowed a conflict between England and Russia for Asiatic supremacy the echoes of which would ring from pole to pole.

Fate decreed otherwise. A war far more wide-spread and terrible than anything we dreamt of in the nineteenth century for Asia has convulsed the world, and for three years found England and Russia on the same side. In the interval Russia had become our friend stage by stage, not only in Asiatic but in world policy, though it took some years, even after 1905, both for frontier officials and average Indian observers to fully realise the change. Still recognition of the transformation had become general in the East before the fateful days of July and August, 1914.

The most unforeseen results have followed. The gigantic and apparently solid Empire of the Tsars had feet of clay. To change the metaphor : it was a reed that broke and pierced the hands that leaned thereon. Few observers in Western Europe realised before the war the real position. But to the Germans, with their commercial activity in Russia, their scientific system of espionage and observation, and spirit of aggressive calculation, the helpless weakness of Russia and its terrible internal divisions were apparent. It was known in Berlin that behind the veneer of Western culture in Petrograd and Moscow there was an ignorance equal to that of any Asiatic country, together with an indolence more reprehensible than that of the negro races. As early as 1900 I heard Germans of high station foretell an inevitable break-up of Russia within the next twenty or thirty years, and indeed immediately should she be foolish enough to go to war against her compact and highly organised neighbour.

I was often in Russia in the years immediately before the war, and observations there excited my surprise that the idea of her prestige was so strong and flattering in Western Europe. At Kiev and elsewhere in South-Western Russia I heard Ukrainians —the people who have always hated the name of "Little Russia"—constantly declare that they were a heavily oppressed people, and that their one thought was to break away from the Tsar's dominions on the first opportunity. Austrian intrigue was rampant, and the Ruthenes of Galicia acted as the outpost of Westernism. In Poland no one, whether prince or peasant, made a secret of the fact that the Poles had an enemy in Russia, and that they would break away on the first occasion that offered. Riga was in fact if not in theory a German city, and in particular the western portions of the Baltic provinces had more sympathy and similarity with the institutions and races of Prussia than with those of the Muscovites. In the early stages of the war I failed to understand the great fear of Russia expressed by my Mahomedan friends and compatriots, who seemed to look upon her prospective occupation of Constantinople as the dawn of Slav world dominion.

The aftermath of the Russian Revolution has proved that the Germans were right in their estimate of their northern neighbour, and that Western Europe was mistaken in fondly showering its gold and energy upon her. Whatever the issue may be, the great Power that threatened India in the nineteenth century is a thing of the past : the Romanoffs are as dead politically as the Mogul dynasty. But the weakness and break-up of Russia is no theme for Indian complacency. Like China in her impotence, what was the Northern Empire is now in her dismembered state as great a danger to the world as in her most aggressive moods of the past. The problem of Central Asia and of the Caucasus is not solved, but takes a new and far more disquieting aspect.

CHAPTER XV

GERMANY'S ASIATIC AMBITIONS

THE new orientation following on the collapse of Russian resistance to the Central Powers along the Eastern front profoundly affects the balance of forces in the Middle East, and though there are many elements of uncertainty in the tangle of international affairs which cannot be unravelled until the war is ended, our present study must take account of the possibilities thus opened up. At the time of writing there are no signs of that return of military strength and political cohesion for Russia which optimistic writers, hoping against hope, have thought possible. With Germany's dominance established in the western provinces of what was Russia, in Ukrainia and the waters of the Black Sea, her ally Turkey once more becomes, whatever the future of Syria or Mesopotamia may be, a powerful Asiatic State with great possibilities of influence. The terms of peace imposed on Russia revived the hopes of the German people in many directions, but no part of the Brest-Litovsk instrument more stirred their imagination than that which opened up new and enlarged visions of Oriental penetration. No one can read the treaties with the Bolshevists and the Ukraine in the most summary fashion without being impressed by the clauses in which Germany insists on the national independence of Persia and Afghanistan, and on her unfettered access to those countries.[1]

So far as paper guarantees go Persia's position as a sovereign power was already assured, as attested by her signature of various international instruments at the Hague and elsewhere. Afghanistan, on the other hand, had no place at the council table of the nations, for while in everything else a full sovereign State, she was debarred from foreign relations except through and with the British Government established in India. The object of Germany in bringing both countries within the terms of the peace she exacted from Russia is obvious. She wishes to extend her influence and her so-called protectorate over these Moslem States, and thus to range them with Turkey. And behind these immediate aims there is a still greater objective. As was pointed out by Lord Lamington, a strenuous friend of Persian independence, shortly before publication of the Brest-Litovsk Treaty, Germany does not restrict her vision to developing the natural resources of that country. Her aims are not only commercial, but military and territorial. "If Germany were successful in attaining this end, it would constitute a grave and constant menace to the security of India; it would be, in fact, a *point d'appui* against our Pacific dominions and Eastern possessions."[2]

It is worth while in this connection to recall the manner and methods by which the Wilhelmstrasse

[1] Article VII of the Brest-Litovsk Treaty reads: "Starting from the fact that Persia and Afghanistan are free and independent States, the contracting parties undertake to respect their political and economic independence and territorial integrity."

[2] *Pall Mall Gazette*, 27 February, 1918.

succeeded in establishing a virtual protectorate over Turkey, and how British influence, historically great at the Porte, came to an end. That influence survived Mr. Gladstone's fierce denunciations of Turkish misrule of subject races. The late Sultan Abdul Hamid knew how to play off one Great Power against another, but was by no means an unenthusiastic admirer of England. As late as January, 1901, in the course of a long audience with which he honoured me at the palace of Yildiz, he dropped the observation that he was confident the British Navy would come to the help of Turkey if she were in a tight corner.

Critics of the foreign policy of the Liberal Government of 1906 onwards have insisted since the breakdown of Russia that when Lord Salisbury talked of Britain's backing the wrong horse in the Crimean War he was himself wrong; that the policy of Canning, of Palmerston, and of Beaconsfield was right, and that if we had put our money on the Ottoman instead of the Muscovite horse we would have done better alike for ourselves and for mankind. Then, at the outbreak of the Great War, these critics maintain, the Porte would have remained under British influence, and Germany's way to the East would have been blocked from the start. It is urged that Russian inefficiency was an open book, her internal racial differences an historical fact to which our statesmen closed their eyes. This criticism could be justified on the assumption that the Liberal Government had a free and open choice in the selection of a favourite starter in the diplomatic race. No such choice was open to Viscount Grey of Falloden. We can well believe that the Asquith Government desired to be the friends and protectors of Turkey, and to retain the position they acquired after the first Young Turk Revolution. It was not unfriendliness, but fear of opposition from both Russia and Germany which prevented the loan of British and Anglo-Indian officers to Turkey to reorganise her Asiatic provinces. Nor was it a matter of mere light-hearted choice that led to the British loss of commanding influence at Constantinople.

To comprehend the developments of world policy since the dawn of our century, we must go back to its infant years, and remember what had then become a fundamental principle of German policy, namely, that it was within the power of the Germanic States to be the dominating factor in world politics. This was no mere sentiment of the Court and the Wilhelmstrasse, or the military and ruling sets. All classes, even the barbers, waiters, and shopmen who crowded Western Europe, shared the feeling, whether consciously or semi-consciously. We read this in a hundred signs and portents, in manifold disclosures in the last four years, and not least in the hundreds of thousands of men and women of all classes subscribing in peace days to that militant organisation the German Navy League, the spirit of which has been incarnated since the sword was drawn by Admiral von Tirpitz and his Pan-German followers. Whatever the policy pursued by the Asquith Government had been (and we know from the confidential Lichnowsky memorandum, published without the consent of the ex-Ambassador in London, how earnestly they sought peace and ensued it to the last minute of the eleventh hour) it is a foregone conclusion that Germany would have taken up the opposite line of policy. An understanding in due perspective of the many-threaded woof and web of European diplomacy in the first fourteen years of the century is impossible without keeping steadily in mind the cardinal consideration that the other Powers, both great and small, were but potential seconds and thirds in the inevitable duel of which Britain and Germany were to be the principals. These respective rôles have been maintained throughout the war, and in all its phases. It is Britain and her far-flung dominions, guarded by an unconquered Navy, which have blocked the way year after year of the quick victorious decision on which the Kaiser and his advisers so confidently reckoned.

The real choice before the Asquith Government eight or ten years ago was either to take up the moral protection of Turkey, leaving Germany to bring Russia under her influence and to repeat the formation of the Drei Kaiserbund; or to ally herself with France and Russia and draw the Entente closer, leaving to Germany the protection of Turkey from traditional Muscovite ambitions. Had Britain backed the Turkish horse she would have been faced with the fact that France, the natural counterpoise to Germany in Europe, was the ally of Russia. However mistakenly, the French Government in and beyond the first decade of the century relied more on the so-called Colossus than on their Channel neighbour. Hence there would have been danger of France either refusing the responsibility of offending her old Russian Ally by adopting a pro-Turkish policy in order to meet the wishes of Whitehall; or still worse, of the

Republic being drawn, in spite of the bitter memories of 1870, toward Germany. In that event the Continental alliance against England dreamt of by impatient Pan-Germans at certain stages of the Boer War, would have taken life and shape on substantial foundations.

Nor would this alternative policy have insured Britain's route to the East from serious menace. The history of the Eastern question points to the probability that under such conditions Russia would have attacked Turkey, after a settlement of terms with Berlin and Vienna. This is what happened in 1877. No one who has carefully read the history of the last Russo-Turkish war can deny that Alexander II, before sending his troops into Ottoman territories received the consent of his uncle at Potsdam, and that Bismarck was fully apprised of Russian intentions. It is well known that before the declaration of war, a meeting took place, at Bismarck's suggestion, between Alexander II and Francis Joseph and Andrassy. It resulted in a secret settlement by which Russia was to compensate herself in Trans-Caucasia and free Bulgaria, while Austria received the Turkish provinces of Bosnia and Herzegovina, nominally under a trusteeship. Their annexation by the Dual Monarchy ten years ago, in disregard of the terms of the Berlin Treaty, was the first step toward the cynical breach of international compacts by the Central Powers to which they were parties, whenever it has suited their purpose to treat them as mere "scraps of paper." Had English policy in recent years been directed to the protection of Turkey, rather than to the development of the Entente, we should have seen almost a repetition of the experiences of forty years ago. It is highly probable that the Tsar, with the Kaiser's consent, would have come to an arrangement by which Austria would have absorbed European Turkey up to Salonika, and Russia would have established herself at the Golden Horn. This would not have been inconsistent with the ultimate aims of the Wilhelmstrasse in the direction of world dominion. Germany's share in the bargain would have been a free hand in the West, and a secret certainty of being able later to turn against Russia with the help of her brilliant second, Austria, thus mastering the East after having gained and consolidated the hegemony of the West of the Continent.

Confronted by these alternatives, Lord Grey and Mr. Asquith pursued a policy which had great dangers, as the war has shown, but of the two it was the more prudent. The consequences of Turkey falling into the hands of Germany could not have been wholly unforeseen, although the risk was taken, since the alternative policy would have been still more perilous. To-day we must face fairly and squarely the issues arising from the subordination of the Porte to Berlin, as affected by the Russian collapse. Whatever the reverberating effect of Japanese intervention in the Far East may be, Russian weakness and internal divisions (including the fact that the Russians were only a part of the nation that went under the name of Russia, and had forced their supremacy under Peter the Great and his successors on their unwilling and more civilised Polish and Lettish subjects of the West) leave it a practical certainty that Germano-Turkish influence in the Near East will have to be reckoned with by British statesmanship after the war. In the Middle East alone will Britain be in a position to set up a strong barrier against the extension of that influence East and South. Her successes in Palestine and Mesopotamia are enormously in her favour in this respect, and she is not hampered by any instrument, such as that the Foreign Office was prepared to make, as Prince Lichnowsky tells us, in the fateful summer of 1914. By the treaty then on the point of signature, says the ex-Ambassador, "the whole of Mesopotamia up to Basra became our zone of interest, whereby the whole British rights, the question of shipping on the Tigris, and the Wilcox establishments were left untouched, as well as all the district of Baghdad, and the Anatolian railways."

In both Persia and Afghanistan we find non-Turanian races, with their own culture and history, with their national character and with interests which ought to be the same as those of England, provided she disabuses the minds of her diplomatists amd officials of being always and on every occasion the predominant partners and superiors. Before we approach either Afghanistan or Persia with friendly assistance Britain must set her face against resort in those regions to the methods by which Egypt is governed. Even amongst the Arabs of Mesopotamia and Syria, with every cause to welcome the overthrow of Turkish rule, the traditions of real self-determination are so strong that they will be grievously disappointed if release from the heavy yoke is replaced by a just but still alien domination—if their countries, like Egypt, become mere conquered lands governed from above by the fiat of a foreign bureaucracy. The Oriental nations may have been wanting in the passionate yet reasoned patriotism of their European contemporaries. Yet they are sensitive, and the sensitiveness increases with their education and culture. No civilised peoples care to be mere ciphers of European Chancelleries, or at best what the late Lord Cromer called them—native hands to be directed by European heads.

The South Persia Rifles, which have done such good work in most difficult conditions under Brigadier-General Sir Percy Sykes in the last two years, and any forces by which they may be supplemented, will require careful, tactful, and determined supervision, lest they should degenerate into corps paid for by Persia and owned by Britain, similar to the Hyderabad Contingent, until it was absorbed in the Indian Army by the agreement with the late Nizam in 1902. Care must be taken that, unlike the Egyptian Army organised by Englishmen since the occupation, the South Persia Rifles bear in mind that the Shah is their real sovereign and that Persian interests must be dominant. Happily this consideration will be thoroughly appreciated by an officer so familiar with, and sympathetic toward, Persian life and thought as Sir Percy Sykes, and the War Cabinet is pledged to the observance of the principle.[1] Still,

[1] "The force [South Persia Rifles] continued to be what it was in its inception, what it will, I hope, always remain—namely, a Persian force. The most assiduous attempts have been made by pro-German elements, with whose devices we are now so familiar, to represent this force as a part of the British or Indian Army, and as engaged in a military occupation of the country. Of course, it is nothing of the sort, it is Persian in character, composition, and allegiance, and the first to suffer from its disappearance would be Persia herself. . . . We desire Persia to remain neutral during the war, and to retain her complete independence after the war. There should be no difficulty in finding a solution to the question

it may easily be overlooked as time goes on by a nation which has had so much experience as Great Britain of ruling other races. Its disregard, whether in letter or spirit, would be a potent means of diverting Persian sympathy to Turkey and Germany.

What is true of Persia will be equally true of Afghanistan under the changed conditions. The present arrangement is ideal so long as that country has an independent sovereign, and the non-British world leaves it and the North-West frontier of India alone. The Afghans enjoy absolute Home Rule of the autocratic type, and their government, whatever we in the West may think of it, is in accord with their own wishes and history. H.M. the Ameer has kept his royal word; in spite of pressure from some hot-headed advisers and of Turco-German intrigues and embassies, he has been a true friend of Britain in these years of world conflagration. His fidelity has contributed very largely to the averting of any general rising of the tribes of the North-West frontier like that of 1897–8. His policy has been conservative in the best sense of the term. He has shown the world that the national interests of which he is the guardian come first and last in his consideration, and that the tinsel ambitions set before him by intriguers do not divert him from the wise path of concentration bequeathed by his strong father. But even in his dominions the present situation, however advantageous to those immediately concerned, the Afghans and the British Government,

[of the future of the force after the war] that will fulfil the triple criterion of satisfying Persian national sentiments, providing for the safety of the roads, and protecting the legitimate interests of trade."—LORD CURZON, House of Lords, 21 January, 1918.

cannot go on for ever. World forces draw the West to the East, and also the East to the West. Sooner or later the time must come when the Afghan, like the Persian and the Turk, will need the help of a powerful but sincere friend.

Under the changing conditions of our times, the maintenance of British supremacy in Asia is bound up, in my conviction, with the exercise of such true friendship toward Persia and Afghanistan without any ulterior purpose of mastering those countries in practice, whatever the name and outward form of the relationship. However great our detestation of German fraud and trickery may be, there is something at least to be learned from pre-war events in Constantinople as to the dealings of an European Power with an Oriental country. The lesson is that of the possibility of acquiring great influence among Eastern peoples without violating their self-respect or leading them to be apprehensive as to the maintenance of their independence. The new way of helping independent Oriental countries will mean, on the part of British diplomatic officers, the jettisoning of many traditions, other than the best, and the learning of new lessons. There is, in fact, no alternative policy, except actual acquisition by Britain, for preventing Persia and Afghanistan from ultimately falling under German influence.

Apart from the moral side of the question, which no one with responsibility and influence in King George's dominions ought to forget, there is a grave practical obstacle to absorption. The acquisition of the two great countries of the Middle East, and their administration after the manner applied to Egypt since the Occupation, would tax

England's powers almost to breaking-point. It would be an immense addition to Imperial burdens, inevitably augmented as these have been by the war. Its immorality, open or disguised, could but engender loss of Britain's great moral prestige in the East. It is to be remembered that Great Britain, which has sincerely disclaimed any rivalry to German ambitions of the hegemony of the world, cannot indefinitely add to her manifold commitments. Lord Salisbury once met Jingo pressure by the characteristic observation that if the Government yielded to every argument of this kind Great Britain would be forced to annex the moon in order to prevent an attack from Mars. I am not concerned here to define the limits to be set; but if friendly relations with Persia and Afghanistan, with Mesopotamia and Arabia, specially Southern and Eastern, are developed in correspondence with their respective claims to self-determination, we can look without alarm, if not with indifference, on events in parts of Asia more remote from India and our route thither. The policy here advocated would make of Persia and Afghanistan, through no other bond than self-interest, firm and fast friends. What is needed is that Englishmen should be ready to take service under the Shah or the Ameer as educationists, as military instructors, as scientists, as doctors, and in other capacities with single-minded loyalty to those countries and their rulers. Sir Salter Pyne, for many years Chief Engineer to the late Ameer Abdur Rahman Khan, set an excellent example of the right attitude in such service.

The good name of England in the East, however, requires as a great object lesson and at the first possible opportunity the liberalising of the administration of Egypt, for this is long overdue. The position of the Sultan of that country and its people, their political helplessness—compared to which the Native States and even British India enjoy full liberty—tend to give Great Britain a bad name in the East, since they offer her enemies a ready example in impressing on the Orient ideas of British territorial selfishness and race pride. The very material prosperity our laws, our irrigation works, and our equitable fiscal system have brought has served to emphasise the political and intellectual, the moral and spiritual backwardness of the Egyptians, *vis à vis* the officials. At the end of the war it ought not to be difficult to evolve an administration of the Protectorate more in keeping with modern ideas everywhere, including the East. Nothing would do more to raise the real prestige of Britain for liberalism than a thorough reform of the Egyptian administration by a far larger infusion of native co-operation, and the grant of greater powers alike to the Sultan, to the Egyptian Ministers, and to popularly elected assemblies for both national and local municipal purposes. In these days when just stress is laid in the principle of self-determination such a corollary to the contemplated political advances in India would enormously increase the Eastern belief in British honour and beneficence.

A sincere policy of assisting both Persia and Afghanistan in the onward march which modern conditions demand, will raise two natural ramparts for India in the North-West that neither German nor Slav, Turk nor Mongol, can ever hope to destroy. They will be drawn of their own accord toward the Power which provides the object lesson of a healthy form of federalism in India, with real autonomy for each province, with the internal freedom of principalities assured, with a revived and liberalised kingdom of Hyderabad, including the Berars, under the Nizam. They would see in India freedom and order, autonomy, and yet Imperial union, and would appreciate for themselves the advantages of a confederation assuring the continuance of internal self-government buttressed by goodwill, the immense and unlimited strength of that great Empire on which the sun never sets. The British position in Mesopotamia and Arabia also, whatever its nominal form may be, would be infinitely strengthened by the policy I have advocated.

CHAPTER XVI

ISLAMIC AND TURANIAN MOVEMENTS

THE Great War has disposed, once for all, of a modern international bogey. In the early eighties, when Turkey had just emerged from her disastrous encounter with Russia, her European misfortunes were followed by still greater losses in Africa. Her shadowy protection over Tunis was replaced by French rule; and Egypt, through the bungling of its rulers as well as of the late Sultan Abdul Hamid, was metamorphosed in fact if not in name, into a British possession. In Asia, the Arab tribes were increasingly restive. In such circumstances the late Professor Arminius Vambéry, the Hungarian Orientalist, and other Europeans who had the entrée of the Court of Abdul Hamid, let drop words and ideas that led the Sultan into his main political dream of Pan-Islamism. From that day forward, mullahs, fakirs, and other zealous emissaries were all over Asia and Africa preaching the reunion of Islam under Constantinople. The Sultan was encouraged by the astrologer Abdul Huda, as well as by Afghan and Persian readers of portents. Even after the downfall of Hamidism, the Young Turks continued this policy for some years.

Political Pan-Islamism had its foundations on sand, and could not endure. There is a right and legitimate Pan-Islamism to which every sincere and believing Mahomedan belongs—that is, the theory of the spiritual brotherhood and unity of the children of the Prophet. It is a deep, perennial element in that Perso-Arabian culture, that great family of civilisation to which we gave the name Islamic in the first chapter. It connotes charity and goodwill toward fellow-believers everywhere from China to Morocco, from the Volga to Singapore. It means an abiding interest in the literature of Islam, in her beautiful arts, in her lovely architecture, in her entrancing poetry. It also means a true reformation—a return to the early and pure simplicity of the faith, to its preaching by persuasion and argument, to the manifestation of a spiritual power in individual lives, to beneficent activity for mankind. This natural and worthy spiritual movement makes not only the Master and His teaching but also His children of all climes an object of affection to the Turk or the Afghan, to the Indian or the Egyptian. A famine or a desolating fire in the Moslem quarters of Kashgar or Sarajevo would immediately draw the sympathy and material assistance of the Mahomedan of Delhi or Cairo. The real spiritual and cultural unity of Islam must ever grow, for to the follower of the Prophet it is the foundation of the life of the soul.

The spread of this spiritual and cultural Pan-Islamism, this true religion of brotherhood and affection, in our time has been promoted by the facilities of modern civilisation, by the growth of the spirit of liberty, and by the general awakening of the East which began late in the nineteenth century. It had nothing to do with and nothing to receive from the Court of Stamboul. The hopeless theory entertained by Abdul Hamid of reaching political unity among such scattered and different nationalities was as futile as it would be for the Pope of Rome to dream of gathering the Catholics throughout the world under a common temporal sovereignty. This political Pan-Islamism of the late Sultan was finally swept away on the outbreak of the Great War. Religion has more and more become a spiritual force in the modern world, and less and less a temporal one. In this war national and material interests have predominated over religious ties. The sturdy Protestantism of England and America has come to grips with the Lutherism of Germany and the Calvinism of Hungary. Catholic Austria and Catholic Italy are arch enemies. The Jews of every country have been loyal to the flags of their respective lands.

The same feature has been observable in Islam. But here new aspirations arose. Whether through personal and dynastic ambition or through deeper racial feelings of antipathy, many of the ruling families of the Arabian Peninsula have broken away from Turkey, notwithstanding all the bonds of religion. An independent Arabian monarchy has arisen in Hedjaz and has helped to clear the Red Sea coast of Turkish troops. Just as the Moslem Albanians were eager to obtain autonomy, so the Moslem Arabs have evinced tendencies toward racial home rule. Whether a united Arabian nationality will once again be reared is a question that no man living can answer.

The one thing clear is that the break-up of the Russian Empire and the disappearance of Hamidian and political Pan-Islamism have revealed a new problem. Like the German and Slav dreams of national unity this political force, though brought into prominence by events, is not a thing of yesterday. The vast majority of the Russian Moslems are of Turko-Tartar origin and language. In the Caucasus and in Persia there is a large Turkish-speaking Turanian element. The eighties saw a literary movement begun both in Constantinople and in Asiatic Russia toward a cultural and linguistic rapprochement of the Anatolians and the other branches of the Turanian family. The preliminary efforts were toward grammatical and linguistic renovation, as well as toward bringing out both prose and poetry on modern European principles, to replace the Persian and Arabic metre but in as pure Turkish as possible.

After the still-born Russian revolution of 1905 and the coming into power of the Young Turk, sources of communication and of sympathy grew. With the outbreak of the world war, and the resulting disappointment of the Porte with the failure of political Pan-Islamism, as shown by the Arab revolt, the governing classes in Turkey turned their hopes eastwards towards their Russo-Persian cousins. Perso-Arabic words were more and more dropped, alike in Turkey and amongst the other branches of the Turanian races, and the names of Mongol heroes were more and more given to children. Such cognomens as Jenghiz, Timur, Baber, Mangu, Ordoghrol, and Hulagu were made fashionable. It is not improbable that when peace is restored Turkey will seek to exert much greater influence than hitherto over communities of related origin in the Caucasus, on the shores of the Volga, and in Central Asia. The same may be said as to her ambitions in relation to the Turki tribes of Persia.

By way of the Sublime Porte, therefore, Germany will endeavour to exercise a powerful influence in the Middle East. This serious contingency has to be faced; but I cherish the assurance that if England is true to her traditional principles of liberty, and respect for national aspirations, there will be no danger of her influence in Asia being successfully challenged. A satisfied, autonomous India, an Afghanistan and a Persia whose independence and future are ensured, and receiving from England such economic, commercial, and cultural assistance as an independent country can have from stronger neighbours without humiliation—these will be far too strong, alike in moral and material forces, to fear anything from the Turanian races of Northern Asia.

Though Germano-Turkish influence is reaching Central Asia, in no part of the Middle East will it find the resources either in men or material to give any chance of attacking the foundations of British dominion in Asia, provided the peoples who go to make up, in the widest sense, these spheres of British influence are satisfied and happy. If we carry out the wise internal policy of founding true national self-government through federalism of all the greater races of India; if sincere friendship toward Afghanistan is developed; if toward Persia we follow a genuine policy of helpfulness without any *arrière-pensée* of reducing her right to a national and free government, or making of her a second and impotent Egypt—given these conditions we may be quite sure that the South Asiatic Federation, with England as its friend, protector, and pivot, will be strong enough to meet any aggression, whether from Germanised Turkey or Japan.

The converse proposition may be stated with equal emphasis. The outlook would be most depressing if we took the wrong road of excessive centralisation by an impossible attempt at unilateral instead of federal government in a free India; of reducing Persian independence to a position like that of Egypt or Morocco; or of unjustified humiliation of the Afghan national pride. We should thus travel in the direction of reducing the symbol of Britain to the level of that of the Muscovite Tsar. The body politic would be inoculated with the germs of disease, such as would make India in the long run an easy prey to a combination of attack from without and sedition from within. In modern as well as ancient times great empires not built on the stable foundations of freedom, nationality, and justice, have broken down from the blows of smaller but healthier neighbours. It is for us to follow the moral, genuinely disinterested and nation-conserving policy that will make the free South Asiatic Federation of to-morrow one of the great dominions of that free union of nations of which Britain is the heart and the King-Emperor the beloved head.

CHAPTER XVII

THE PATH TO WIDER CONFEDERATION

OUR survey of international problems affecting India's neighbours may be followed by tracing in fuller detail the intimate connection between satisfactory progress in relations with them and the principles on which Indian constitutional advances, even those of the immediate future, are based. From this and other standpoints, the use of the term "responsible government" instead of "self-government" by Mr. Montagu in the historic announcement to the House of Commons on August 20, 1917, is to be regretted. We know from Lord Curzon (House of Lords, 24th October, 1917) that the terms of the announcement were the subject of "repeated discussion at the Cabinet," and I am convinced that the words "responsible government" were used in order to carry with the Secretaty of State and the Prime Minister some more conservative members of the small War Cabinet. It was employed so that the Executive Government hereafter might contain Englishmen, while at the same time the administration became sufficiently liberal to be responsible to the people. The adjective is unfortunate because it carries the technical meaning of a government responsible for its existence to an assembly elected by the people. On the other hand, "self-government" can comprise many and varied forms of expression of the popular will.

Responsible government, in the narrow and technical sense in which Mr. Montagu's announcement is being interpreted in some quarters, has been really successful alone in the United Kingdom, and there only up to a certain point. In England the two-party system, quite inconceivable in India, was held years ago by no less a judge of constitutional history than Bagehot to have been the real cause of the success of this form of government. But in the words of a competent observer to-day "the breakdown of Parliamentary government, which had become increasingly acute in the years preceding the war, was due to the fact that the British people had persisted in attempting in one Parliament and with one executive to deal with three classes of business," viz. Imperial affairs; questions affecting the United Kingdom as a whole; and the internal affairs of the three countries.[1] Under the stress of war conditions, many of the traditional elements of responsibility of the executive to Parliament are in suspense.

In France, where, for historical reasons, there are many parties, this principle has led to unstable guidance and constant changes in ministries, and has brought to the front in public life a kaleidoscopic crowd of individuals instead of a few outstanding national characters. France is a very great nation, but a sincere admirer who loves her almost

[1] Letter to the *Times*, 5 February, 1918, by Lord Hythe (now Earl Brassey) urging the necessity for a federal form of government in the United Kingdom, both on grounds of efficiency and to provide the one effective solution of the Irish Home Rule problem. This view has gained widespread acceptance since the issue of the Irish Convention report.

as a foster-mother country may be allowed to say that she is great in spite of her governmental system. Sympathetic students of the French Constitution, such as Mr. Bodley, and passionate French patriots, such as M. Déroulède, have regretted that the immediate fear of Cæsarism led the founders of the Third Republic to adopt the English model instead of that of the other great Anglo-Saxon State.

In Spain this narrow "responsible" form of constitution has led, as it must in any half-educated country where parliamentary institutions are not a tradition of the people, to Rotativism, which, though nominally responsible to the electorate, is the very negation of good government. At this moment, heroic efforts are being made to do away with the system. So long as Portugal was a constitutional monarchy, the same hopeless plan of Rotativism strangled her development; since her change to republicanism constant revolutions and unrest have succeeded the former national inactivity. In Greece, until Venizelos, a man of genius, came to the head of affairs, the reality without the name of Rotativism held sway and nearly ruined that small but gifted people.

On the other hand, who will be so foolish as to say that the United States of America are not composed of self-governing communities? Who will allege that the Federal Government at Washington is not in the truest sense a government of the people, by the people, and for the people? Yet the system by which it exists is diametrically opposed to "responsible government" in the narrow sense. The executive is even more separate and independent of the legislature than in Germany. There the leading ministers are always nominated by the King of Prussia as Prussia's representatives to the Federal Council; and thus, in a roundabout way by belonging to the Upper House, they come into contact with the popular assembly. In America Cabinet Ministers are entirely responsible to the President, and, by the Constitution at least, have no more influence or part in the acts of the legislature than any ordinary private citizen. Nor are they, as in Germany, of practical necessity members of the Senate.

It would be a disaster for India to be forced into the narrow form of constitutionalism that developed with its essential condition of two great rival parties, in England through historical and natural causes, but is now confessedly in need of reform. Mere imitation of features of the British Constitution, we have seen, has had most disillusioning results in the Iberian Peninsula and in Greece. It is true that a form of responsibility to parliament has succeeded in the Northern States of Europe; but here it must be remembered that in Sweden, the most important of the three Scandinavian Governments, the system is a half-way house between responsibility as understood in England, and the German practice of separation of powers as between the executive and the legislative bodies. Constitutional government has succeeded only where it has been cast in a form natural to the history and development of the people. In America, with all fidelity to democratic principles, it has taken forms widely different from those of Great Britain. In Japan, also, it is in practice anything but a slavish imitation of the English methods. Indeed, it is nearer to the Swedish than to any other system existing in the West. In Germany and Austria it approaches the American system, though the partition between the executive and the legislature is not so marked.

Why should India be forced to imitate a system of government evolved through many centuries in a geographically small country with two historical parties? Why should India be placed on this Procrustean bed, instead of allowing the more widely elected legislature and an executive with a century and a half of tradition behind it to develop naturally their own inner working, just as they have been evolved in other countries? We want self-government, we want responsible government in the widest sense of the term—that of ultimate responsibility to the people—but we do not want our nascent national institutions to be put into swaddling clothes because one word instead of another was chosen by the British War Cabinet for its public declaration. The Indian peoples, with an instinctive sense of their need, have asked for self-government within the Empire, not for parliamentary institutions on the British model. None of the draft schemes prepared by Indians from that of Gokhale to the joint representation of the National Congress and the Moslem League hypothecate full and immediate responsibility of the executive to the legislature.

It is an unfair and prejudiced criticism of the federal form of government to argue that the free provincial parliaments will be nothing but glorified municipalities. Surely autonomy for our great provinces, with populations of from twenty to fifty millions, with their vast and varied lands, each equal in natural resources to one of the greater European

States, is a sufficient field for the ambition and devotion of any patriot. It must be remembered that as true federalists we advocate for the government of each of the great province-states the same measure of ultimate internal independence from the central authorities as is now enjoyed by the Nizam or the Rajput princes over their own territories.

This brings me to the first of two questions I wish to put to the critics of federalism as here advocated. By what other system can the Native States be brought into active union with the rest of India ? No scheme of reconstruction can be complete without taking into consideration the 70,000,000 people and the 710,000 square miles comprised within these areas scattered all over India. Can these lands remain permanently out of touch with the great reconstructed India of the future ? Or, as an alternative, are we to tear up treaties that assured their princes full autonomy within their respective spheres ? Or is it seriously maintained that the central Government, while scrupulously avoiding interference in any question relating to a tiny principality or its court, should at the same time control the great province-states from Simla or Delhi, as if they were nothing but so many territories occupied by superior forces ? The history of the past, no less than the justice and symmetry to be sought to-day, leads to the conclusion that we need a federation which can be entered by the greatest provinces and the smallest Native Raj alike without loss of internal freedom, and yet with the assurance that, in all federal matters, they will pull together for a united Empire.

Under the system I have advocated, with its checks, balances, and safeguards, there can be little danger of any province falling into misgovernment. It is common ground with students of Indian affairs that a State like Mysore should have full control of internal policy. If this principle holds good of an essentially non-democratic régime, why should it not apply to our great national states, where legislative and financial control is finally vested in a representative assembly, and where the immovable executive is strong enough to carry out measures of justice and utility?

The second question for the advocate of a unilateral system to ponder is that of the effect on the international future in Asia. An outstanding tendency in the political ferment of to-day is for small nations, while retaining their individuality, to gather to a central, powerful State that carries them along in a common course. In recent years the United States have drawn into their orbit many of the smaller entities of the New World, such as Cuba and the republics of Central America. Germany has Austria, Turkey and Bulgaria ranged with her, and she is ambitious to secure within her sphere of influence the States that have been surrendered through the Bolshevist betrayal of Russia. She dreams of ultimately bringing Holland and Flanders, Denmark, Norway and Sweden, and even Switzerland within her constellation. England and France and Italy have now taken a common route in world politics, carrying with them many wide-flung dominions. Even the three Scandinavian monarchies, free as they ordinarily are from the bewildering entanglements of world-politics, have found that practical independence can only be maintained by greater union and cohesion. We have to-day, in fact, a common North European policy, into which the new Republic of Finland longs to be drawn. It has been ruthlessly invaded because it forms a barrier to Teutonic ambitions in North Western Europe. But the most competent observers are agreed that whatever changes peace may bring, Germany will not turn away her eyes from Middle Asia.

It is for the Indian patriot to recognise that Persia, Afghanistan, and possibly Arabia must sooner or later come within the orbit of some Continental Power—such as Germany, or what may grow out of the break-up of Russia—or must throw in their lot with that of the Indian Empire, with which they have so much more genuine affinity. The world forces that move small states into closer contact with powerful neighbours, though so far most visible in Europe, will inevitably make themselves felt in Asia. Unless she is willing to accept the prospect of having powerful and possibly inimical neighbours to watch, and the heavy military burdens thereby entailed, India cannot afford to neglect to draw her Mahomedan neighbour states to herself by the ties of mutual interest and goodwill.

A lesson of the Great War that even Germany has been reluctantly compelled to recognise is that force, though remorselessly applied by her military leaders, is insufficient to secure the incorporation of weakened nations. In Courland, in Lithuania, in Flanders herself, German policy has wavered between merciless severity and efforts to win the hearts of such elements of the population as the Flemings and the Baltes to her *kultur* and interests.

British policy ought to have no such conflict of ideals. Hence it is unthinkable that the British Empire can pursue a course of mere conquest in the Middle East. Such a policy is foreign to her ideals and repugnant to her interests. It would be more disastrous for England and India than almost anything else I can conceive, for it would mean the violation of the principles of humanity and justice, and would provoke continued unrest. On the other hand, a merely negative attitude will not meet the dangers I have indicated. We must have a policy attractive enough to draw toward our centre State the outer nations. A system of federation, just to each member, united by ties of common interest, would serve as a magnet for them. It would be a great harbour light for any weak state of the Middle East.

Once the internal federation was complete and the economic influence northwards and westwards developed, we might expect the Afghans themselves to seek association therein. The fact that Bengal and Bombay, Hyderabad and Kashmir were enjoying full autonomy, would be a guarantee to the Afghans of no risk of loss of independence in entering the federation. Just as the indigenous rulers of Rajputna would have their place, there is no reason why a group of principalities from Arabia and the Southern littoral of the Persian Gulf, should not ultimately become members of the union that will ensure peace and liberty, freedom and order to the south of Asia. Subsequently, Persia herself would be attracted, and just as the natural pride of Bavaria or Saxony has not been diminished by inclusion within the German Union, so, on a greater and more difficult but happily beneficent basis, the empire of Persia and the kingdom of Afghanistan could honourably enter a federation of which Delhi would be the centre.

Needless to say, no compulsion, direct or indirect, can be employed. The right course is to institute such a type of community of states as to draw the sympathy and practical interest of India's neighbours. The magnet would attract, as time went on, the isolated and remote lands of Nepal, Bhutan, and Tibet. The Crown Colony of Ceylon naturally and historically belongs to India. She is cut off from the mainland by a mere geological accident, and the shallow channels and intermittent rocks that divide her therefrom are already partly, and will soon be completely, bridged by the Indo-Ceylon Railway. A unilateral government of India could have no attraction for the people of the island. They would naturally prefer being governed from Whitehall rather than Delhi, for Whitehall, being so much further away, interferes less, while the Parliamentary institutions of England afford Ceylon guarantees in normal times against injustice and needless mandates from without. The autonomous system would give the *coup de grâce* to the pleas put forward from time to time for the separation of Burma from the Indian Empire, which spring from dissatisfaction with the present centralised control.

In a word, the path of beneficent and growing union must be based on a federal India, with every member exercising her individual rights, her historic peculiarities and natural interests, yet protected by a common defensive system and customs union from external danger and economic exploitation by stronger forces. Such a federal India would promptly bring Ceylon to the bosom of her natural mother, and the further developments we have indicated would follow. We can build a great South Asiatic federation by now laying the foundations wide and deep on justice, on liberty, and on recognition for every race, every religion, and every historical entity.

CHAPTER XVIII

ARMY AND NAVY

OUR study of a federated India would be inadequate if it did not take into account the desirable or possible effects on the problems of defence. For generations now the Army in India has consisted of two distinct portions, the one composed of the "white garrison" sojourning in India, and the other recruited within the country or in her border lands. The need for the continuance of a British contingent in the future is generally recognised. England will not be prepared, or indeed able, to leave the defence of India to her own children for many years to come. Nor is it desirable that premature attempts in this direction should be made, both because the tradition of an Imperial Army in India can develop only slowly, and because the standard of efficiency in British units will continue to afford a great example to the officers and men of the Indian Army.

The events of the last four years, however, will lead inevitably to reconstruction and readjustment. Till the outbreak of the Great War, Lord Cardwell's military system, in essentials at least, remained supreme in Britain, although great changes were made while peace remained by the Haldane reorganisation on a territorial basis. The linked battalion system since Cardwell's day has made it a matter of easy arrangement to send troops to India for given periods of service and to maintain their drafts. Many observers believe that in the light of these searching experiences in a war engaging the great bulk of her young manhood, England, instead of returning to her former military arrangements and standards, will organise a short service national system. It is difficult to see how such a system could meet the special needs of the British Army in India. It will be for the military authorities to consider whether this requirement can be met by contingents, such as, I believe, Dilke recommended, of long service men recruited for the East alone, or whether some other plan is preferable.

Whatever the system adopted may be, I am convinced that the supreme command of the British as well as of the Indian section of the Army in India must be held by a Commander-in-Chief and staff located in the country. The concentration of command in Whitehall, advocated by some observers on account of the breakdown of organisation in Mesopotamia in 1915–16, could not make for efficiency. There would be lack of unity of control of contingents working side by side and engaged in a common purpose. Since India naturally benefits by the presence of the British garrison, she will continue to pay for its maintenance. Hence control by the War Office would be an injustice. India will rightly claim that the direction and supervision of all troops in the country, whether British or Indian, shall be in the hands of a Commander-in-Chief on the spot.

To clearly understand the position of the indigenous Indian Army, we must look back to its inception and the fundamental ideas of the originators. Though Clive was the main creator of this asset in the British struggle for supremacy, the underlying ideas were those of Dupleix, whose remarkable genius and immense abilities were never fully recognised by France. Long familiarity with the results have led to forgetfulness of the originality of Dupleix's conception. So far, the history of the mediæval and modern world has shown only two striking and successful methods of raising foreign troops for conquest when national forces were not strong enough or sufficiently within reach for the purpose. The first of these was the old Turkish system of Janissaries, created in the fourteenth century, and constituting the tribute of children from the conquered Christians, whose upbringing and discipline were undertaken by the State. This militia rapidly contributed to the subjugation of the Christian States in Eastern Europe; and it increased the numbers of the Turkish nation, since it absorbed the children of conquered peoples.

The other method, happily devoid of elements of individual enslavement and injustice, but also based on the principle of ruling other people through the agency of forces supplied by themselves, was conceived in the master brain of Dupleix. It was that of raising, disciplining, paying, and officering through Europeans Indian forces on a large scale and using them for the conquest of their own countrymen. Clive, Stringer Lawrence, and other military geniuses of the East India Company carried out the plan thoroughly, but the authorities are agreed that the original idea was that of the far-sighted Frenchman who made a strong bid for the supremacy of his country in India.[1] The Native Army in India, up to a few years ago, was, in principle, still based on his conception of a body of troops for keeping the country to which they belong under the rule of their foreign masters, or the furtherance, by the absorption of troublesome neighbouring States, or the prevention of aggression from without, of the same foreign rule. The beneficence of that rule alike in intention and act did not eliminate this fundamental conception, though it destroyed the theory that India was held merely by the sword.

The first notable change in conception, though technically a verbal one only, came when at the Durbar in 1903 the name of these forces was changed from the "Native" to the "Indian" Army. It received a national and territorial basis, instead of being merely a racially different auxiliary of the British forces holding the country. A much more radical breach in the old idea was made when Mr. Montagu announced on August, 20th, 1917, the removal of the bar which had previously precluded the admission of Indians to higher commissioned rank in His Majesty's Army, and that such commissions were to be granted to nine Indian officers who had served in the field in the present war, and had been recommended for the honour by the

[1] "The raising of actual native regiments was first undertaken by the French, and it was due to the coming struggle for mastery and Southern India that we owe the first conception of a regular native army. In 1748 Dupleix raised several battalions of Musalman soldiery armed in the European fashion in the Carnatic, and a few years later Stringer Lawrence followed suit in Madras."—*The Armies of India,* by Major G. F. MacMunn. London, 1911.

"It is, indeed, hardly too much to say that we owe our native army to France."—*Imperial Gazetteer of India,* Vol. IV, p. 326. Oxford, 1907.

Government of India in recognition of their services.

Thus the first steps had been taken toward making the Indian Army a truly national force, like the armies of any normal country in any part of the world. For its development hereafter deep and strong foundations will be necessary. We have to make of the military sons of India a great central national entity, a truly Imperial force above all local or other jealousies. As long as can now be foreseen, English officers will be necessary in the Indian Army; but an early step must be the establishment of one or two great military schools in India, open alike to the subjects of Native States and of the British provinces, for the training of officers. At the same time, Indian officers of the old school who have shown ability and resource should be occasionally raised to the higher commissioned ranks. Every province and every race should be eligible to contribute to the make-up of the Army, and a short service system—short, that is, for India—of four or five years, with twelve years in the reserve, should become general. Such an army would be a national and a uniting force, and must be trusted fully by the Imperial authorities. This war must have proved to the least imaginative observer that any policy of mistrust is a cruel libel on the sentiments of the people. There would be religious and caste company organisation, and whole regiments would be formed on the same basis if found necessary; but the Army would be exclusively under the control of the Viceroy and the central executive. It would be a trained Imperial force ready to be sent wherever the needs of Empire required.

If we are to have the unity of control that is so essential, and if India is to develop on sound federal principles, the Native States must be prepared to make a sacrifice, by surrendering their present right of maintaining troops, so that all units raised should form part of the Imperial forces, with similar conditions of service, promotion, etc. The princes would lose little in reality, for even now the best of their troops are Imperial Service contingents. The opening of the door to higher commissioned rank has removed one of the obstacles to unification, since there will now be scope for the employment of Native State officers in responsible work in the Imperial Army. Nor need there be any break with the traditions of territorial origin. In England, in Germany, and in many other countries, each provincial or county regiment bears the name of its area of recruitment, and carries emblems of its own history. Similarly, forces raised in the Punjab, or in Bengal, would carry appropriate symbols, while regiments raised in Native States would proudly bear the emblems of the reigning house, and would be under the honorary command of the ruling prince. The fundamental point is that in policy, in discipline, in movement, in everything that goes to the making of an efficient defensive force, there must be a uniform and federal army for the whole of India. The time has come to establish not only proper Indian artillery on a scale in keeping with the interests to be defended, but to make the country more completely self-contained in respect to all branches of equipment, and not least for the provision of aircraft and other scientific inventions in which such great advances have been made during the war. It is highly satisfactory to know that rapid progress in this direction is resulting from the activities of the Indian Munitions Board, under the energetic and widely informed chairmanship of Sir Thomas Holland.

As a necessary compliment to the short service system, a territorial militia or reserve should be established, of which those who have gone through the mill of the active Army would naturally form the main element. But care must be taken to ensure the absolute and complete control of the central Government over the Territorials, no less than over the Regulars. The old problem of the relations of the civil and military powers, so acutely raised by the Kitchener-Curzon controversy in 1905 and again brought into prominence by the findings of the Mesopotamian Commission, can perhaps be best solved by establishing a Ministry of War, with a soldier occupant. This would leave the Commander-in-Chief free to devote himself to the problems of strategy and military efficiency and of field inspection.

I cannot leave this part of the subject of defence without emphasising one of the vital conditions of satisfactory progress already indicated. It is that there should be no barrier to army service on the mere ground of race or religion. India's contribution of man power to the Great War, immense though its value has been, has been hampered by the narrow conceptions of a former and now distant day. In the words of a well-informed observer, "It is now recognised by the most conservative experts, in the light of war experiences, that the demarcation between martial and non-martial races in India has been too rigidly drawn."[1] The time has come for unreserved acceptance of the principle partly recognised in what is at present a mere skeleton Indian Defence Force, laid down by Sir Satyendra Sinha from the chair of the 30th Indian National Congress, held at Bombay in December, 1915, that Indians should be entitled "to enlist in the Regular Army, irrespective of race or province of origin, but subject only to prescribed tests of physical fitness." On such tests the Madrasi or Bengali should be as eligible, so far as the regulations are concerned, as the Sikh or the Rajput. It must not be forgotten that on many battlefields the troops of Madras and Bengal did magnificent service in the eighteenth century in helping to secure British dominance in India. From those presidencies the Indian Army mainly originated.[2]

[1] *The Times*, Educational Supplement, 31st January, 1918.

[2] Since writing this chapter I have read with hearty appreciation the memorandum submitted to the Secretary of State and the Viceroy by my friend Sir Ibrahim Rahimtula, who has now succeeded Sir M. B. Chaubal as a member of the Bombay Government. As the *Times of India* observes, he at least is not of the "large number of estimable publicists in India who honestly believe that after this war we can beat our swords into ploughshares and our bayonets into chaupatti-turners." Emphasising the changed outlook on defensive problems which the scientific advances stimulated by the war have brought, Sir Ibrahim lays down the sound principle that each of the great units of the Empire should be sufficiently self-contained for the purposes of defence to stand against any sudden attack and keep the enemy at bay till the Armies and Navies of other parts of the Empire can come to its help. He urges that the number of fighting men in India should be largely increased: "There is a superabundance of man-power in India, not only sufficient for the defence of the country, but also for the rest of the Empire. Most of the difficulties which Britain has had to contend with, during the present war, would have never arisen if full confidence had been reposed in the undoubted loyalty of India and a large Indian Army had been trained for the defence of the Empire. It is not too late even now. Britain has to recognise that India is and has always been whole-hearted in her loyalty to the British Crown. . . . Whether Government decide to increase the Indian

Command of the sea has been a vital element in the unimpaired maintenance of British supremacy. Under the East India Company's rule, the Indian Navy, manned by the seafaring communities of the great peninsula and officered by Englishmen, roamed all over the Eastern seas. It took part in many a naval fight, and piracy in Western Asia was suppressed by its constant activities. Its end came only with the completion of its work. The Royal Navy entirely replaced that of the Company in 1862, except for transport, police, survey, and other local duties discharged by the Royal Indian Marine. Thus for nearly two generations India has been dependent for maritime defence on the Navy voted by the House of Commons and maintained by the British Exchequer. Even before the war there were close students of naval strategy and history who urged that the system, necessary as it had been, was becoming antiquated, and that there was growing need for the upbuilding of a strong Indian Navy.

The arguments on this head of the late Commander C. R. Low, the historian of the old Indian Navy, and other writers have gained fresh force and validity in the upheavals of the last four years. The wonderful resources of England have

Army on a permanent basis, or whether some such system as a national second line is adopted, there does not appear to me to be any doubt that the response will be more than adequate. The best course would probably be to adopt both the systems side by side and thus reduce the cost of maintenance of the large fighting force required. The first line Army though more effective is very costly, and it appears to me unnecessary to keep the entire force required for purposes of defence on that basis. A system under which a large number of men, following different vocations in life, can and should be requisitioned for the purpose of training, to be called up when necessary in the defence of their country, will appeal to every patriotic Indian."—*Times of India*, 26 January, 1918.

been exposed to enormous strain, much of it continuous in character, and there will be many pressing demands upon them when peace has been signed. It seems to me unreasonable to expect Great Britain to bear the entire burden of keeping the Eastern seas clear. The sacrifices of the war have fallen lightly on the Far Eastern Power which has contributed to the naval work of the Allies; indeed their pressure, until the question of military intervention in Siberia arose this year, had been negligible in comparison with the rapid development of her industries and overseas commerce for which opportunity has been provided by the martial and armament-making preoccupations of the great countries fully sharing in the fight on both land and sea. Japan has had a fine economic opportunity, and has utilised it to the utmost. The Anglo-Japanese Alliance has worked so smoothly during this century that it has been easy to forget the sense in which India has been dependent on the continued goodwill of the Empire of the Rising Sun. However well intentioned, faithful to her treaty obligations, and conservative in the best sense this progressive Asiatic Power may be, it is not fitting that India should be dependent on the forbearance of any great nation, no matter how friendly and helpful. The strange mutations of foreign relations are written large in the history of the world in the last half-dozen years, and have to be provided against.

The need for tonnage to replace the very serious wastages arising from Germany's remorseless submarine campaign will be one of the great problems of reconstruction for the next twenty years. With this, also, India must help to cope. In the days of

John Company the ships built in her yards sailed in all the seas, and were known in every great port. There is no reason why this tradition should not be revived under the impetus of a pressing need and with the greatly improved facilities of modern industrial science. If India is to possess a merchant fleet of her own, she must protect it within her legitimate sphere of ocean influence by a proper defence organisation. I shall have more to say on the subject when discussing the material development of the country.

An easy, but most unfortunate, arrangement would be for India to contribute to the cost of the Royal Navy, thus limiting her share in Imperial maritime defence to the mere payment of subventions. Wise statesmanship will be careful to avoid a policy which would be the more distasteful since it would place India on a different footing to that of the self-governing dominions. If the Indian quota lacked the Swadeshi element, it would soon be represented as a burdensome addition to taxation, since there would be little to bring home to the people of the country the necessity for sharing in the naval price of Empire. Moreover, the need of Britain in the many-sided work of reconstruction after the war will be not only for money but for men. The Eastern Navy would fittingly be recruited in the East, and its headquarters should also be there. I do not dispute the cogency of the strategical reasons for the measures of naval concentration taken in the last few years of peace; but the fact remains that the depredations of the *Emden* in the early months of the war provided an object lesson as to the considerable harm a single hostile raider may be able to commit when the Eastern seas are largely denuded of protection.[1]

For the success of the proposed system two methods of recruitment and training will be required. Britain will have to loan to India the services of a considerable number of naval officers to instruct young Indians of good family in a professional college established at Bombay, Karachi, or Madras. Concurrently steps must be taken to provide the rank and file for the future Indian Navy from amongst the seafaring population of the coast, that now supplies so many units of the British mercantile marine with excellent sailors. The existing small naval yards in India would be enlarged, and others would be provided, to undertake, at first, the construction of submarines and light cruisers, and ultimately the most advanced of capital ships that can be built.

Such an Indian Navy, apart from its direct utility, would be a unifying force amongst the provinces and nationalities sharing the responsibility for its maintenance. It would be Imperial in the truest sense. With its sister forces sure to be developed from present beginnings, namely, the navies of Australia and South Africa, it would be charged with upholding British supremacy in the Pacific and Indian Oceans, leaving the United

[1] I note with satisfaction that Sir Ibrahim Rahimtula's memorandum is as emphatic on the naval as on the military need. For the defence of the extensive sea-coast of India he holds it necessary "that there should be in Indian waters sufficient material for naval defence." He also advocates measures to secure for the country a sufficient mercantile marine. He recognises the heavy cost of these defensive measures; but he approaches the question from the guiding standpoint "that whatever the cost, the alternative of remaining in a state of unpreparedness is so brimful of evils, especially having regard to the Asiatic situation, that the problem has to be boldly faced."—*Times of India*, 26 January, 1918.

Kingdom free for the concurrent task of its maintenance in European waters, and, with the help of Canada, in the Atlantic. It is to be earnestly hoped that not only the mere beginning, but a clearly thought-out plan for these naval developments will be formulated without delay, so that when peace comes some of the many naval men of various ratings who would otherwise be paid off may be offered employment in connection with the foundation of a new Indian Navy destined to far surpass the finest traditions of its predecessor of early Victorian times.

CHAPTER XIX

INDUSTRIES AND TARIFFS

FROM the consideration of the constitution, framework, and official agency, civil and defensive, of Indian government, and of the relations of the sub-continent to the rest of the Empire and neighbouring States, we pass to the outlook for the material development required to enable India to take the high place in the economic life of the Empire to which she is entitled by the extent and variety of her potential resources, and the labour of her vast and industrious population. We can sketch the subject only in broad outline, for anything like a complete summary of the situation, present and prospective, would require a volume to itself. It is difficult to avoid mere banalities in a general reference; but to leave this immense problem untouched would make our study of the Indian renaissance so incomplete as to be misleading.

In the broadest sense of the term India is still economically a "plantation." Her fields, her forests, her jungles, and her mines yield materials of many kinds and qualities needed both in crude and developed forms for her own population and also in demand from outside markets; but hitherto she has derived benefit too exclusively from the raw and unfinished form of her products. The war has given a very notable impulse to Indian industry. As Mr. Austen Chamberlain recently pointed out,[1] the Government and the people have been stimulated to develop and make use of their own resources. While the external demand for many Indian products has rapidly grown, they have been forced to look around and see how far they could provide for themselves articles, or substitutes for articles, hitherto obtained from abroad. But I am sure that no one would be more ready than Sir Thomas Holland, the energetic and resourceful president of the Indian Munitions Board and chairman of the Industries Commission, to admit that we still are in the early stages of the industrial expansion of the country.

A feather shows the direction of the wind, and conditions before the war can be indicated by a small yet significant instance. India is a great wheat-exporting country; yet the usual brands of biscuits in demand there were imported. Such anomalies confronted one at every turn; a large proportion of "Europe goods" in the shops were manufactured from Indian raw materials, or else were well within the range of local Indian enterprise. Even to-day, with the great steel industry which the genius and foresight of the late Jamsetjee Tata and the patriotic enterprise of his sons have established at Sakchi, the full development of this essential industry in Southern Asia is far from accomplishment. No country, however great or favourably situated, can be completely self-supporting in her industries, and the ideal in a

[1] Speech from the chair at meeting of Indian Section, Royal Society of Arts, 14 March, 1918.

real League of Nations would be for each State to produce what is most congenial to her soil and conditions and then to allow free exchange to lead to the use by all mankind of the fruits of the whole earth. But India, like the United States, with her varied climate and immense extent, can come as near a complete variety of production as it is desirable for any country with great trade interests abroad to possess.

As a first step to this end, her Government and people ought to have the power of being able to develop, as freely as Canada or Australia, the industries that are most in need of encouragement. No amount of political evolution will meet the necessities of the country unless it includes fiscal independence entrusted to the Government of India and the Senate representing all the provinces and principalities. The arguments to which we were accustomed in pre-war days for maintaining Free Trade in the United Kingdom are exactly the opposite of those by which a system of free imports for India could be supported. In Great Britain the question of protection has centred round the taxation of imported corn on the one hand and of maintaining relatively cheap raw materials for manufactures on the other. India's exports are almost entirely foodstuffs and raw materials A scientific schedule would give her rulers the power of taxing those imports that are the luxuries of the rich or that can be naturally and advantageously developed in India. The present *ad valorem* system is anything but scientific, and in some directions it heavily handicaps Indian manufacturing development.

Nothing has contributed more to the strength and unanimity of Indian feeling on this subject than the favour shown to Lancashire in the incidence of customs duties since their general re-imposition nearly a quarter of a century ago—a preference dictated from Whitehall as the result of political pressure. The countervailing excise duty on the products of the Indian mills was officially defended on a plea of principle, namely, that in order to ensure the non-protective character of the "revenue" tariff, "an excise tax, equivalent to the amount of import duty, should be imposed on the products of any industry in India which showed signs of sufficient development to compete with goods from abroad."[1] But the theory completely broke down by virtue of its application to the cotton industry alone, which had behind it in Great Britain a sufficient Parliamentary representation to decide the fate of Ministers not possessing an overwhelming majority of votes in the House of Commons. India owes a great debt to Mr. Austen Chamberlain for so courageously facing Lancashire opposition in bringing the tariff on imported cotton goods to the general level of 7½ per cent, without a corresponding rise in the excise duty on the products of the Indian mills, thus making a 4 per cent differentiation. Lord Hardinge, in his memorandum appealing to the Secretary of State for the excise duty to be abolished, or at any rate for no increase to be made therein when the import duty was raised, said that the time had come to "abolish a purely adventitious piece of injustice." It is important to remember that the injustice, while so deeply felt in

[1] The *Times*-Trade Supplement, India Section, February, 1918.

India as to be "a running sore," extended at least in minor degree to other British manufactures, competing with Indian-made goods.[1]

We are promised a reconsideration of the Government of India's recommendation for the abolition of the countervailing excise when the war is over. Besides this tardy act of justice, attention should be paid without delay to the general effect of the *ad valorem* system of duties in operating against industrial development. One result of the general increase in the tariff from 5 to 7½ per cent made in 1916 was to curtail considerably the schedule of goods entitled to exemption from duty. Up to that time practically all machinery except that worked by manual or animal labour was duty free. Now the only motor power machines entitled to exemption are those imported by owners of cotton-spinning or weaving mills. For the benefit of agriculture various machines for field and barn, when constructed so that they can be worked by animal or manual labour, are on the free list. But there is a very wide range of costly plant for industrial purposes paying 2½ per cent duty, including all machinery (other than that on the free list, worked by non-manual or animal power);

[1] "The House must not and will not suppose that the Government of India in this matter are exposing one British trade to exceptional disabilities. On the contrary, even when this has been done, the cotton trade of Lancashire is treated more favourably in India than any other British industry. . . . It was for the cotton industry alone that any excise was imposed. The duties on other British products were raised from 5 to 7½ per cent last year, and no voice was raised, as far as I know, inside or outside this House to say that I and my right hon. friend were in a plot to break the party truce or carry out some nefarious and dark plan. All that we are doing to-day is in some partial degree to assimilate the treatment of Lancashire with the treatment of other manufactured goods which enter India."—Mr. AUSTEN CHAMBERLAIN, House of Commons, 14 March, 1917.

component parts of such machinery; and all iron and steel castings, bars, rods, and constructional material; also railway plant, and apparatus and appliances imported by railway companies.[1]

In the sphere of India's greatest industry, agriculture, the system operates against development. Motor engines and steam tractors are essential to the progress with which I deal in a subsequent chapter. India must either produce these instruments in great quantities, or must import them on a vast scale. If she is to build them herself, she must have the machinery for their construction; but the customs duty comes in the way and artificially raises the price of such machinery. If she imports the motor engines and steam tractors the case becomes worse, for then machinery of prime necessity to her agriculture is directly taxed, which comes to the same thing as an indirect tax on food.

The time has come for India to adjust her tariff system to her own interests and those of the Empire as a whole. Modern history shows how vital to material progress is the power of such adjustment. When Japan won her political emancipation, she placed fiscal independence in the forefront of her programme even before the abolition of "capitulations." During the year immediately preceding the present war, the foreign relations of Turkey with the Great Powers were marked by her continual attempt to free herself from an *ad valorem* and general system of import duties, and to introduce a scientific tariff. The United States, the Argentine, and the German

[1] The great rise in prices resulting from the war increases the discouraging effect of the system on industrial progress.

Empire, each possessing scientific customs schedules, made extraordinary progress during the last decades of the nineteenth century and the beginning of the twentieth. In Russia, owing to the want of political liberty and the concentration of power in the hands of a clique absorbed in the policy of preservation of its authority, customs dues were enforced, not for the benefit of national industries, but for artificially raising revenue of prices. The tariff stood in the way of economic development, and undoubtedly contributed to the discontent that brought about the Revolution and its disastrous consequences.

CHAPTER XX

CREDIT AND COMMERCE

THERE is practically no limit to Indian industrial progress given an appropriate tariff, the steady and earnest encouragement of the State, and complete abandonment of the old policy of *laisser faire, laisser aller.* To take but a few instances in a thousand, India, with her palms and sugar canes, with the possibility of growing almost every kind of nut, should be able to manufacture sugar, margarine, and industrial oils, not only for her own growing requirements, but also in sufficient quantities to go far to supply the needs of the Europe of to-morrow. When all the waterfalls of the mountain chains of the two southern coasts and of the central plateau are brought into active use—and in this direction notable beginnings have been made—the poorest of the peasantry ought to have within reach a supply of electric power such as is known now only in the happiest districts of Switzerland. The Tata Hydro-Electric Works have already provided for the factories of Bombay cheap electric power which has gone far to substitute a clean form of motive power for the furnaces by which soot and dirt are spread through India's most beautiful city. It is not too much to say that the commercial utilisation of the opportunities for introducing water power in all suitable areas would increase the cotton industry alone fivefold. The jute and tea industries, mainly in British hands, ought to serve as outstanding examples for the enterprise and capital of the Indian people. The vast chain of the Himalayas, with its innumerable waterfalls, offers the possibility of a long line of industrial garden cities from Kashmir to Bhutan. The great peninsula provides an ideal field for commercial pisciculture. The waters of the Indian Ocean and of the Bay of Bengal are rich in all kinds of salt-water fish; the great internal waterways need scientific culture of fresh-water fish. The industry might become comparable with that of Scandinavia, providing, with the use of Indian vegetable oils, for the more widespread and economical dietary of fish that would do much to bring health and strength to the people.

It has to be admitted that at present public confidence in joint-stock enterprise is not great. For one thing the history of banking and co-operative capitalism in India has not been fortunate. The extraordinary and absurdly speculative Share Mania of the 'sixties in Western India deterred thousands of well-to-do people from participation in joint-stock effort. Half a century later, in the period immediately preceding the war, the series of Swadeshi banking failures, at a time when the country was not going through any economic crisis, frightened away an overwhelmingly greater number of potential investors than had participated in furnishing unsound banking concerns with funds. The experience of modern Germany goes to show that full economic development depends, among other things, upon a satisfactory banking system, working hand in hand with the manufacturer and the trader. France, though great and rich, has been wanting in such co-operation. Hence, instead of employing her capital on the sure and remunerative foundation of manufactures on her own soil, she was led by the great centralised banking corporations in Paris to loan it to such bad debtors as Russia, Turkey, Bulgaria, and Mexico.

In India our banking facilities are not only very limited; they retain in essentials the general character of half a century ago, that of slender financial aid and supervision to the large export and import trade which, whatever else happens, must always go on. The facilities are amazingly inadequate. Throughout the whole Indian Empire there are banks or branches of banks in only 153 towns—an average location of rather less than one place for banking for every 2,000,000 inhabitants. Four out of every five towns with a population of 10,000 and over are without any branch of a joint-stock bank.[1] The Tata group has now established an industrial bank which will be of great advantage in promoting manufacturing enterprise. The provision of a central State bank has often been discussed. Whether the State can fittingly help to meet the present lack of facilities by starting corporations throughout the country, receiving the capital at fixed rates of interest and advancing it to manufacturers, with the right of audit and inspection of their books, is well worth careful consideration. What the State can certainly do is to encourage the increase of facilities by non-official agency by the many indirect means at its disposal. In the United States the provincial banks are the backbone of industry and commerce, and yet are looked upon as semi-national institutions.

[1] Statistical Tables Relating to Banks in India. Third Issue, 1917.

Financial confidence is a tender plant in a country like India, and this consideration should lead to a small but significant modification of the policy of Government. Under the famous Regulation of 1818 giving powers of deportation, and also under various provisions of our own day for strengthening the hands of Government against sedition, there is authority to confiscate the property of political offenders. Although the power is very rarely used, its existence, independently of judicial decision after public trial, checks the growth of that full confidence which, in England, or in America, or Germany, is evident in the stability of business enterprise. I cannot forget that when the Natu Brothers were arrested in Poona by the fiat of Lord Sandhurst's Government, and their property was taken into the custody of the State, there were many signs that a real blow had been struck at the confidence of people who had never had anything to do with politics. Men met in little groups with long faces, and remarks were common as to the insecurity of property in a country where a small council in camera, and on police evidence, could deprive individuals not only of their liberty but of possessions for which perhaps generations of their family had laboured.

I am well aware that instances of actual confiscation are so infrequent that the " prestige " school of Anglo-Indians might consider my contention far-fetched. But from personal observation I do not hesitate to say that such a reserve power has considerable influence in encouraging secret hoarding in place of investment. I have constantly heard non-political and conservative people refer to this absolute power as a reason for hiding, or sending abroad, their money and for failing to take opportunities for placing it out at good interest. So long as the State does not renounce such arbitrary authority, it cannot expect from its subjects the full confidence that will lead to their loaning money to the State or to joint-stock enterprise. Frederick II long ago laid down for Prussian administration the principle that whatever was done with the life and liberty of the people, property should be sacred, and should not be touched except through obviously fair processes of law and trial. I cannot imagine any measure that would give more thorough confidence in India than a formal and legal enactment that in no circumstances could property be taken from a criminal or a revolutionary as a matter of punishment, save in the shape of fines prescribed by law. It is an axiom of justice that the crime of the individual should be punished on his person or by an immediate demand on his income and not by the confiscation of property which ultimately benefits his dependents.

Communications, in the widest sense of the term, have a most important part to play in the co-operation the State can provide for business enterprise and development. It will be necessary under the constitution proposed in these pages for the railway rates to be constantly studied by the responsible department of the central Government, and to be varied and arranged to encourage alike the exports and imports required for national development of wealth. It is not inevitable that remote places should wait interminably for railway communication. A motor traction service must be started in areas where, for the present, the elaborate railway system would not pay. Cheap telephones, which, with the immense water-power India has at command should be in widespread use, will lead to greater expansion by facilitating business intercourse. In some parts of the country greater use can be made of the inland waterways.

These internal communications, however, will fail in completeness unless they are supplemented and fed by a national commercial fleet. India now depends entirely on a few British lines of steamers, and on small coasters and sailing vessels. The excellent example set by the famous ship-owning family in Bombay of which Sir Yusof Soudagar is now the distinguished head, was not followed, and India has lost the place she once occupied as a ship-building country. The scarcity of world tonnage occasioned by Germany's inhuman submarine campaign and the war requirements of the Allies has had the inevitable effect of some effort to recover India's lost capacity in this respect. No feature of the work of the Indian Munitions Board is more welcome than the recent organisation of a ship-building branch, which is expected to construct vessels up to 1600 tons, in addition to the construction and re-erection of river craft and the supply of accessory materials for the inland water transport of Mesopotamia. This beginning must not be allowed to lack development when the war is over. Unless a nation, like Britain, has for generations excelled in maritime communications, raising large capital for the purpose, and has gained commercial prestige and experience on a scale impossible for a new-comer, it seems doubtful whether, without State aid in the shape of bounties, a great commercial fleet can be provided, having regard to the experience of Germany, France, Austria, and Italy. When the Government of India is relieved of its needless and microscopic examination of what the already elaborate provincial Governments have done, it will be free to study important problems such as the measure of State aid required to give Indian commerce and industry those maritime appliances without which the trade equipment of a peninsular nation is incomplete.

In every foreign country, and especially those of commercial importance, Indians ought to be attached to the staffs of the British Consulates, as representing Indian commercial interests, to provide information and prepare data for bringing foreign exporters and importers into touch with India's possibilities, and *vice versa*. The Imperial Consuls, with the immense work of Britain already on their hands, cannot be expected to pay that detailed attention to India's possibilities that a service designed to promote Indian interests would naturally give. That they do not do so is evident from the most cursory study of Consular reports. For the sake of Imperial unity the proposed service, consisting of both Indians and Englishmen, should be attached to the British Consular service, but should be directly responsible to the Indian Government. A significant beginning has been made in this direction by the establishment of a Trade Commissioner for India in the City of London, Mr. D. T. Chadwick, I.C.S., who is directly responsible to the Government of India and not to the Secretary of State. It is to be hoped that the success of the organisation will lead without delay to similar representation of India in other countries, and not least in the self-governing Dominions.

Such a State organisation, however, will not suffice for India to occupy to the full her proper place in world trade. As Japan found out long ago, it will be necessary for her own manufacturers to establish houses in Europe and America. Thus India will have a second string to her bow, instead of depending solely on the orders of representatives in India of foreign houses. Far more important is the spread of education and knowledge, and general improvement of the sanitary conditions of the homes of the people. Specialised industry needs instructed labour, very different from that which can be supplied by the average ill-fed and ignorant Indian coolie. But education in the widest sense of the term, and national efficiency as required in the modern world, are impossible, as I shall show in another chapter, under an irresponsible and bureaucratic form of government. From its very nature it cannot either fire the imagination of the people or bring home to them the necessity for those greater sacrifices without which, under world conditions to-day, national success is impossible. Any change that does not realise that the classes and castes of India will not take those greater steps except at the behest of their own leaders and under a really national form of government must fail, just as the bureaucracy, plus the present narrow representative system, has failed. So on the grounds of Indian material progress, which is held in some quarters to be jeopardised by a real political advance, I plead for a national system, broadly based on the representation of every class, caste, and creed under the sovereignty of the King-Emperor and within the unity of the Empire.

CHAPTER XXI

AGRICULTURE

WHILE every Indian aspires to see his country taking the high position among the great manufacturing nations of the world outlined in the preceding chapter, the most enthusiastic believers in her industrial development will not deny that, for so long as we can foresee, the exploitation of the surface of the soil must remain the predominating feature of India's economic life, far surpassing all other activities in importance. Following the census definition I include in this category not only farming, but specialised branches of land work such as forestry, fruit growing, pasture, fishing, and hunting. At the last census 69 per cent of the population were dependent upon ordinary cultivation, and 3 per cent on market gardening, the growing of special products, forestry, and the raising of farm stock and small animals.

I could safely challenge any widely travelled and observant fellow-countryman, familiar with social economics on each of the great continents, to deny after due reflection that the present condition of Indian agriculture and of the 219,000,000 human beings dependent thereon is the greatest and most depressing economic tragedy known to him. I readily acknowledge the ameliorative efforts of British rule along certain lines for generations past, such as increasing security of life and property, the lessening by irrigation works of liability to famine in tracts of precarious rainfall, and the evolution of a scientific system of relief works when deficiency of rain has brought on that calamity. But it was not until the present century was well on its way that general, serious, and systematic attempts were made steadily to encourage improvements in agricultural practice. It was left to Lord Curzon, in the closing period of his Viceroyalty, to introduce a definite system for the application of scientific enquiry to the needs of Indian agriculture on a comprehensive basis, and to establish the rural co-operative credit movement.

In the past dozen years these measures may be said to have laid a foundation for all-round advance in agricultural practice. But the distance we have still to travel may be judged by the relatively small effect so far produced on village life. A typical rural scene on an average day in an average year is essentially the same now as it was half a century ago. A breeze, alternately warm and chilly, sweeps over the monotonous landscape as it is lightened by a rapid dawn, to be followed quickly by a heavy molten sun appearing on the horizon. The ill-clad villagers, men, women, and children, thin and weak, and made old beyond their years by a life of under-feeding and over-work, have been astir before daybreak, and have partaken of a scanty meal, consisting of some kind or other of cold porridge, of course without sugar and milk. With bare and hardened feet they reach the fields and immediately begin to furrow the soil with their lean cattle of a poor and hybrid breed, usually sterile and milkless. A short rest at midday, and a handful of dried corn or beans for food, is followed by a continuance till dusk of the same laborious scratching of the soil. Then the weary way homeward in the chilly evening, every member of the family shaking with malaria or fatigue. A drink of water, probably contaminated, the munching of a piece of hard black or green chaupati, a little gossip round the peepul tree, and then the day ends with heavy, unrefreshing sleep in dwellings so insanitary that no decent European farmer would house his cattle in them.

I know of only one other scene of the kind, drawn on a large scale canvas, equally saddening. It is that of an average Great-Russian village before the war, on any day of the seven months of winter there. You would see every man, woman, and child in the village hopelessly drunk, some with open mouths and bewildered expressions, others in a state approaching coma, each family huddled together round the earthen furnace protecting its small wooden cottage from the daily and blinding blizzards. In India, happily for her toilers, the depression is due to physical conditions of want, and not, as in Russia, to moral atrophy caused by the long night of winter when for months the earth is covered by many feet of snow.

In the Indian village the few who can just manage to read or write are regarded with curiosity and awe. The average peasant has not the capacity either to interest himself in recreation or indulge in day-dreams, for grinding labour from childhood and insufficient food have crushed the power of imagination and interest in life out of him. Yet Indian peasants are not temperamentally incapable, as some of the negroes of Africa seem to be, of intellectual and spiritual growth. When, as occasionally happens, the child of an agricultural labourer is brought up under proper care and instruction in a well-to-do urban family, he proves himself almost invariably the mental equal of the boys and girls with whom he plays. He is soon fitted for the surroundings of the best and richest classes, as I have often seen in my mother's house. So no greater moral injustice can be done than to put down to race and climate the economic depression of the Indian peasant to-day.

To teach this vast mass of people better methods of agricultural industry, to awaken in them the ambition for learning and improvement, to lead them to differentiate between waste and thrift when the result is not immediate, to secure for them the just fruits of their toil—these, in the aggregate, constitute the great economic problem of India. The annual value of their tillage, even under present conditions, is estimated at not less than £1,000,000,000, and within the first ten years the activities of the reconstituted and co-ordinated agricultural department, at the great research institute and college at Pusa, and in the provinces, were estimated to have increased the value of the products of the fields by upwards of £2,300,000 per annum.[1] This is no more than a beginning. It is not merely conceivable but certain that, given concentration and national effort on agriculture and subsidiary forms of exploitation of the earth's surface, India could double her economic wealth in the next few years. By further intensive culture

[1] *Agriculture in India*, by James Mackenna, I.C.S., Calcutta, Supt. of Govt. Printing, India. 1915.

I believe she could, long before the end of this generation, treble her wealth and correspondingly raise the standard of living throughout the land.

To this end every branch of the problem must be tackled. Since the forests belong to the State, they can be subjected to further scientific development without any interference with private enterprise. More money and a larger agency must be set aside for safeguarding and utilising this important source of national wealth. The opportunities are vast and varied. Although 22·7 per cent of the area of British India is under the control of the Forest Department, it has been customary to import foreign timber, including railway sleepers, on a large scale.[1]

In agriculture generally the part of a national State, though not so direct, is of still greater importance. A wider distribution of model farms, the constant organisation of agricultural exhibitions in every district, travelling lecturers, special night schools for reading and writing, and, above all, compulsory education of both boys and girls, are the more immediate measures for overcoming ignorance and waste. In respect to improved methods, arrangements have to be made on an enormously larger scale than at present for the supply of suitable and varied seeds, including some of those generally unknown in India; new farm

[1] "This wasteful dependence on outside supplies was partly due to lack of precise information regarding the wonderful forest resources of the country. One prominent import was of Maiyang wood from Siam. It has recently been discovered that the wood is of precisely the same species as the *gurjan* of the Andamans and Chittagong and the *kanyin* of Burma, which are obtainable in adequate quantities at from one-half to one-third of the prices paid for the imported timber."—*The Times* Trade Supplement, April, 1918.

instruments; simple motor and steam engines with men to demonstrate and explain their use; and advances through agricultural banks to allow the peasant to buy them. Intensive agriculture is impossible without a good supply of nitrates, and it is obvious that India cannot afford to buy sufficient quantities from Bolivia and Peru to meet her immense needs. Here we must imitate the resourcefulness of the Germans by establishing scientific laboratories for the production of nitrates from the air. There should be courses of teaching in the economic use and conservation of the common fertilisers of the country, as another essential step for freeing our agriculture from the heavy handicap of want of proper manure.

In respect to the rearing and proper use of farm animals, there is the same disastrous ignorance and want of organisation. To begin with, the value in the national economy of that noble animal, the horse, is far from being realised. Its many uses are either unknown, or known by mere hearsay of what takes place in other countries. The indigenous breed of horses, owing to the lack of those methods which have led to equine improvement in Europe generation after generation, is poor in every sense of the word. Some of the ruling princes have done patriotic work in this direction, but in so immense a country such examples to be effective require extension to every portion of the peninsula, instead of being confined to a few fortunate areas. In some parts of British India English sires have helped occasionally to produce specimens of a superior equine race. The name of Tam-o'-Shanter was a household word in some districts of the Bombay Presidency, and the offspring of that grand old sire are a constant reminder of what can be done. But all this is no more than a beginning. We need sires established in all suitable districts, and scientific studies carried on by veterinaries, so as to bring about in each part of the country those combinations of blood that are most likely to succeed. The English thoroughbred, the Arab stallion, the commoner types of Hungary, Australia, and the Steppes of Russia, and the various kinds of Indian "Kattys" and other special breeds, should be installed all over the country on an adequate scale, with moderate fees for service, and made generally accessible. The peasant, too, must learn the many other uses of the horse than that of an instrument of locomotion.

In the far wider field of cattle breeding, there is need for immediate measures to avert the possibility of something akin to a national economic disaster. All over India we find poor breeds, large numbers of them nothing but emasculated bullocks, eating up the fodder resources. The milk supply is, consequently, poor. There is considerable danger of the few passable breeds disappearing and the multiplication of the unfit. Remedial measures should clearly distinguish the purposes for which we require our bovine herds. If they are mainly for field tillage the time has come to see how far and by what kind of machinery this animal energy can be economically replaced. The proper function of these domestic animals is to provide milk and its many derivatives, and meat, as it is the function of poultry to produce eggs and chickens for the table. And it is in the production of milk and meat that the differences in quality between the best and the inferior cattle are apparent.

Early steps should be taken to study the best mating possible for the native race of cattle in any series of districts owning the same family of cows. The State should set up sufficient bulls to regenerate the breed in as short a time as possible. Again, since the fodder supply is limited—as famine times have tragically shown—every measure must be taken to allow the unfit races to die out. In present conditions the tendency is in the opposite direction. The best breeds, needing greater care and better nourishment, languish and disappear, and the unfit, grazing at times even on the odd growth of quarries, survive. It is true a few choice breeds exist, and here and there earnest friends of the country, notably Lord Willingdon, the Governor of Bombay, have done most valuable service by maintaining special breeds.[1] But these personal endeavours are not in themselves sufficient. An effort on a national scale, with the local officials taking an active part and enlisting the voluntary assistance of the public, is required to raise the standards of cattle in India.

Though less important, the question of the protection and improvement of domestic members of the ovine race must not be neglected. Goat's milk, it is to be remembered, largely takes the place in Asiatic countries of cow's milk. The rearing of goats is less difficult and much cheaper than that of prize cattle; yet national effort is needed not only to maintain the present herds, but to improve the breed and extend their use. In India, as in Asia generally, the pig is little more than a scavenger. Since many Hindus abstain

[1] See His Excellency's interesting description of his cattle farm at Ganeshkhind in the *Agricultural Journal of India*, February, 1918.

from meat on religious grounds and a vast majority are too poor to indulge in it, and since the Mahomedans have the same objection to pork as the Jews, the improvement of the porcine breed is not of great urgency. Yet there are many people who need pigs for various reasons, and it is likely that with rising standards of comfort pork will be in demand from many castes and classes not hitherto using it. Consequently prize sires should be introduced from Europe, and due facilities should be given for the limited extent to which this rural industry can be developed under Indian conditions.

The opportunities on all hands for fruit and vegetable growing have been strangely neglected. I doubt if there is another country in the world where such variety and such excellent quality of these commodities could be produced not only for home consumption but for the overseas markets, alike as fresh and dried foodstuffs. The wide range of climate and soil is such that human enterprise and care alone are needed to revolutionise India's position in this respect. The many Hindu castes which abstain from meat would find in the greater variety of vegetables and fruit obtainable a more wholesome and nourishing dietary. To take one example : the most delicate and delicious asparagus I know (and I have tasted fresh asparagus all over Europe and America) is that which grows easily and with but little cultivation in Kashmir. Yet bottled and tinned Continental and American asparagus is used at table all over India. The products of California could be easily equalled by Northern India, and though the former would continue to lead the way in the American and European markets, there is no reason why India should not hold the premier place in vegetable imports between Egypt and Japan. Excellent cherries, apricots, peaches, pears, apples, and plums of the most varied kind are grown in Baluchistan and the sub-Himalayan districts of Northern India. But so far this has been on so small a scale and with such little skilled supervision that the infant industry has done little more than add new luxuries to the table of the rich. With proper care in cultivation and marketing these fruits could be made familiar articles of sale in fruit and food stores throughout Southern Asia.

Nor is the opportunity confined to the north. On the southern plateaux excellent strawberries, raspberries, and gooseberries are grown. And I have occasionally tasted specimens of high quality pears and peaches grown there, rather as a matter of curiosity than of business effort. The tableland of the Deccan is well suited for the production of many fruits of temperate climates. On the coasts and wherever a natural depression of the soil occurs, delicious tropical fruit can be produced. Given the application of scientific methods there is no reason why India should not supply in addition to her own needs Europe and Australia, Egypt and South Africa, with the best mangoes and mangostines imaginable, with pineapples as good as any ever produced under glass in England, and with a great variety of other delicious though less-known tropical fruit. Some of the best grapes I have tasted, equal to any I have had in Europe or America, have been grown in India, not only in the north, but on the southern plateaux. Here there is opportunity for marketing not only the fresh fruit, but also dried raisins on a large scale. Before the war I could never understand why no effort was made by Indian enterprise to compete with Turkish dried figs in the Anglo-French market.

The cultivation of nuts, now that science has shown how they can be put to a hundred various uses, should become one of the great rural industries of India. In medicinal plants and light food, such as arrowroot, India could easily hold her own against any competitor. But alas ! here, as in so many other directions, general ignorance, want of training, encouragement, and capital, and the inner disorganisation of Indian society have left the peninsula in a position of such dependence on the outer world that she actually imports in finished forms plants that grow wild on her soil in prolific abundance. For instance, Peshawur and Poona, Barrackpore and Bangalore, are capable of each becoming, like Grasse, head-quarters of the scent industry. The most delicious and novel perfume, derived from tropical flowers growing in their neighbourhood, could be manufactured under scientific direction and be sent all over the world. Many of them would have the advantage of being entirely new. Fortunes have been made in France and America and employment has been found for thousands in the industrial use of flowers. In India, where natural conditions are still more favourable, the opportunity is wholly neglected. So far as I am aware there is not a single modern factory for the manufacture of scent in the country.

I will not weary the reader with further evidences of the necessity for making the development of agriculture, in its widest sense, the first and most important economic object of the national reconstitution. For the full attainment of that object State aid is essential, owing in part at least to the economic structure of society. India is the land of a vast peasantry with few large landlords. Even where substantial zemindaris have been evolved by British rule, as notably in Bengal, you do not find the intimate relation of peasant-farmer to proprietor which, in England for instance, is so prominent a feature of the social fabric. The case of France and America is different, for in both countries the farmer is prosperous enough to be able to borrow for improvements on easy terms.

It is to the much-abused class of great landowners that British agriculture owes its maintenance through severe crises to these days of new opportunity. During most of the latter half of the nineteenth century, and especially in the late seventies, the eighties, and early nineties, agrarian depression in England was so great that it seemed quite possible that arable tillage would be abandoned almost entirely, the land being turned, as far as possible, into pasture and grazing commons. The farmer had neither the capital nor the credit to stand against the cycle of depression, and the low scale of wages drove the labourers to town industries. At this critical period the landlords as a class saved British agriculture. Many of them had inherited or saved in better times capital invested in joint-stock enterprise. Others had found scope for activity in commercial and other non-agrarian occupations, some overseas and others in city companies at home. From whatever other sources his capital or income was derived, the average English landlord devoted it to his estates, being traditionally eager to prevent their disintegration. As years went by many of them must have thought the effort hopeless, for they could not have foreseen the rise in prices, and the effect of a gigantic war in putting agriculture on a high pedestal as a patriotic and premier industry, with minimum prices guaranteed by the State over a series of years.

Even in prosperous times the working agriculturist depends to a great extent on the capital of the landlord for improvements, such as drainage, outbuildings, fences, the use of electrical and other labour-saving machines, the better supervision of nitrates. When all the local rates and national taxes are paid, it is doubtful if the average English landlord ever gets more than 3 per cent direct return from the capital invested in his estates. Since the real improvement of the land is far greater than such a narrow return indicates society and the nation secure the greater share of the economic advantage which accrues.

In India the position is entirely different. In the Native States the princes rule their territories, but are not the landlords of great estates. In British India there are great zemindari tracts in Bengal and elsewhere, and the owners ought to do far more from their own resources, generally speaking, than at present for the improvement of farming.[1] But in the English sense of the term landlordship does not exist. Not only in the ryotwari tracts, but also in the less extensive zemindari areas, the ultimate owner is the State. Both in British and in Indian ruled India, the

[1] I note with pleasure the emphasis laid on this duty and that of promoting the general welfare of the tenantry by the Maharaja of Darbangha at a meeting of the newly formed All-India Landholders' Association last February.

so-called landlords are the accidental intermediaries between the owner-State and the lessee-subject. It is for the ultimate owner to advance the capital for improvements.

In the autonomous provinces of the India of to-morrow the great work of the I.C.S. ought to be not alone the carrying on of surveys for settlement of the so-called land tax or rent, but still more, that of guiding and assisting the agricultural banks in making the necessary advances for legitimate and long-overdue improvements. And these banks must constitute, far more than at present, a vitalising agency, ready to advance money, ready to advise improvement, ready to bring the surveyor and the expert to the help of the peasant. In each district there should be a central institution with touring specialists working in hearty co-operation with the agricultural department, and ready to advance money for necessary improvements at quite moderate rates. The advances they make should have a statutory relation to the rates at which Government borrows from the public.

The transformation of India by the concentration of national energy on agricultural advancement will be the main material agency for raising the condition of the people to a reasonable standard within the lifetime of our generation. The provision of large annual loans for the purpose during the next ten years would be justifiable. The autonomous provinces of to-morrow must concentrate on this work of rural regeneration as the greatest executive task before the nation.

CHAPTER XXII

EDUCATION FOR THE MASSES

THE programme of material development sketched in the three preceding chapters will fail of its purpose if the policy of universal and improved education is not adopted and pursued with persistent earnestness. Even those who have but a slight acquaintance with modern India are well aware that it is, with the possible exception of China, the most ignorant of civilised countries. The application of the principles of higher commerce and of scientific agriculture on any general scale are impossible in an almost universal state of intellectual darkness under which the daily labour of life cannot be other than ineffective. The average peasant can learn little or nothing beyond the most routine forms of labour, because his illiteracy leaves him devoid of scope for being taught. A man of genius, though illiterate, such as the Albanian Mahomed Ali, has now and again been found able to govern a country by methods far in advance of the standard it had before reached. But the real tragedy of ignorance is that while it does not prevent the superior individual from reaching full development, it so lowers the standard of the people that it is helpless before superior organisation of any kind.

Most of the ills of India can be ascribed to the

general want of knowledge. Moral and intellectual growth have fallen far behind the material gifts brought by British rule. Indeed, there is something inconsistent between the outward equipment of India, with her roads, railways and irrigation colonies, her armies, her developing industries, her skilled officials, her courts of law, her universities, and her scientists,—and yet with an inward blindness, as deep amongst some of the masses as that of darkest Africa. The particularly modern façade of the building only brings into the stronger relief the intellectual nakedness of those within. The small proportion of literacy to the whole uninstructed mass—59 per thousand at the last census—is appalling; yet it does not represent the real condition of things, for the vast majority of so-called literates have had nothing but the most superficial and fragmentary instruction.[1]

The poverty and disease so general in India is largely attributable to mass ignorance. Even if a Ross or a Rogers discovers means of preventing the most deadly diseases, the unlettered masses cannot be effectively taught to resist the attacks of the invisible and microscopic enemies of their vitality. There is also the terrible waste of energy arising

[1] The Educational Volume of *Statistics of British India* for 1915–16 states that on the average of the last quinquennium only 11 per cent of the pupils in the lower primary stage goes to the upper primary stage. "These figures suggest," says the official record, "that 89 out of every 100 pupils in the lower primary stage never go beyond that stage and receive practically no education." Commenting on this fact in one of its instructive regular Indian articles, the *Times* Educational Supplement (March 14, 1918) says: "It is well known that the scanty instruction received by the great majority of pupils at village schools throughout India does not provide a foundation for subsequent progress. In most cases the children become completely illiterate within ten years of leaving school. It has been calculated that this applies to about 80 per cent of all the village school-children of South India."

from the general incapacity of the untaught to recognise the value of time or to distinguish between economy and waste. From higher standpoints this weight of mental destitution is a grievous handicap. It renders the mass of the people incapable of real spiritual culture and of communion with the Unseen, and tends to degrade religion in all its varied forms to the level of an unreasoning superstition. The whole situation is the more saddening owing to the disproportion of the distribution of literacy among the two sexes. At the last census only ten females per mille were literate, as compared with 106 males. The literacy in English was 95 per 10,000 males, and only one in a thousand females. This means that even in classes and castes where the men have some degree of education, the women are frequently entirely ignorant of the three R's. Since the true culture of the race depends on woman, it follows that the curses of ignorance and superstition are found even in the higher strata of society.

No social duty of the community is more urgent and essential than that of effective educational diffusion. It is sometimes said that the English-educated classes in India have been slow to recognise and press forward the claims of primary instruction. I cannot personally plead guilty to the charge, for throughout my public life I have consistently advocated serious attention to this problem. More than fifteen years have passed since I placed it in the forefront of my humble contribution to the discussion of the Budget in the Imperial Legislature. I expressed regret that year after year went by without serious effort being made from the Imperial Exchequer to raise the standard of intelligence of all classes throughout the country. I asked if it was right in that age of severe economic competition that the vast majority of Indian children should be brought up without possessing even the rudiments of learning.[1]

Again in 1911, taking advantage of the interest in India aroused by the Coronation of His Majesty, and the presence in England of Indian princes and soldiers, I urged in the *National Review* the taking of immediate steps to overcome mass illiteracy in India, and also to reform and extend secondary and higher education. I dealt with the question from the standpoint of the interests not of India alone, but of those of the Empire as a whole. I claimed that this great problem of educational diffusion should not be attacked piecemeal; that in the long run it would be best and cheapest to face the situation boldly at once and to lay out a sufficient sum to meet the main requirements. I went so far as to say that the salvation of India under British rule rested upon the enlightenment of the masses. Its bearing both on Imperial trade development and on an aspect of defence then destined to be of the most crucial importance within a very few years were discussed.[2]

[1] "My Lord, has not the time come for the commencement of some system of universal primary education, such as has been adopted by almost every responsible Government? The extreme poverty of this country has recently been much discussed both here and in England, and all sorts of causes have been found and given to explain the undoubted fact. But, my Lord, in my humble opinion the fundamental cause of this extreme poverty is the ignorance of the great majority of the people. . . . With the ever-present fact that this country is advancing very slowly as compared with Europe and America, has not the time come for taking a bold and generous step towards some system of universal education suited to the conditions of the various provinces of the country?"—East India, Financial Statement for 1903–4. Parliamentary Bluebook No. 151, 1903.

[2] "It is to this, and from this [educational] development of India as part of an Imperial whole that we must look for the means of strengthening

At the time this was written the issue was before the Viceregal Legislature in concrete form. Earlier in the year Gokhale had introduced a Bill "to make better provision for the extension of elementary education," by giving municipalities and local boards permissive power, under various safeguards, to apply compulsion to boys between the ages of six and ten. The opinions of the local Governments were invited, and early in 1912 Gokhale moved that the Bill be referred to a select committee; but this course was officially opposed and the motion was defeated. I think it is now generally recognised that the decision was unfortunate, though it is only fair to say that there was great force in one of the arguments of Sir Harcourt Butler, then Education Member, against the Bill.

her and the Empire at one and the same time. For India must remain one of the pillars of the British Empire—and a most important pillar, because she is to-day the Empire's largest potential market and the greatest reservoir of man-power within the limits of British heritage. That is why the education of her people is so vital: vital because of the future increase of her commerce, vital because of the almost unlimited areas of cultivation within her boundaries, vital because of her defensive strength and as a half-way house to the great self-governing States of South Africa, Australia, and New Zealand. By education there can be trained a people whose past history has proved that they can be fighters and can show a loyalty to their leaders unparalleled in history. Therefore the motto to-day for British and Indian statesmen must be, 'Educate, educate, educate.' Look for a passing moment at the question of man-power. . . . India could put troops into South Africa as quickly as they could be sent from England; she could land soldiers in Australia long before England could do so; and forces from India could reach Western Canada almost as soon as from England. Still more: India from her vast reservoir can supply thousands where England can only send hundreds. . . . If by education the myriads of India can be taught that they are guardians and supporters of the Crown, just as are the white citizens of the Empire, then the realisation that India and the self-governing dominions stand and fall together, bound by a community of interests and a common cause to maintain, will have come. . . . It is imperative to give Indians the education to fit them for their future rôle in the British Empire."—*National Review*, July, 1911.

It was that in a country so vast and so varied in degrees of progress, such legislation ought to be provincial rather than Imperial.

A beginning in this decentralising policy, hitherto rendered difficult by the policy of the Government of India, has now been made. Last year Mr. V. J. Patel obtained sanction for the introduction of a similar, though in important respects a more advanced, measure in the Bombay Legislature. It secured the support of the Government of the liberal and fair-minded Lord Willingdon, and, after careful amendment by a select committee presided over by Sir M. B. Chaubal, was passed into law at the end of last year. The Viceroy subsequently announced that the Government of India have decided not to place obstacles in the way of such provincial legislatures as may decide "on any reasonable measures, whether those are the precise measures which we would ourselves be prepared to initiate or not." Bills after the Bombay pattern have been unofficially introduced in the Bengal and Behar Councils, and in the Punjab the Government have drafted a Bill on comprehensive lines.

These are welcome steps, and it is a matter for keen satisfaction that the principle of compulsion has at last found a place on the Statute-book of British India. But permissive measures, having regard to the slender resources of the local bodies and the present centralisation of State financial control, will not adequately meet the need for a general raising of the standard to be effected within a reasonable period, say the life of the younger members of the present generation. It seems to me that the ideal course is for each local legislature, after autonomous powers have been conferred on the provinces, to make kindergarten and primary instruction compulsory for both sexes, except where want of funds prevents the immediate placing of schools within reach of the population. The advantage of this over the permissive method would be that in every possible place, and to the extent that money was forthcoming, compulsion would take effect. The exceptional and unfortunate districts would be brought within the range of public knowledge and sympathy, and would be in the way of securing the assistance both of public and private funds from without.

If less drastic measures are taken, India will remain handicapped by general ignorance when the economic world position, after the war, provides her with extraordinary opportunities for development. If the problem is played with by leaving the decision to individual localities, largely on the basis of increasing the local rates, we cannot hope to see India attain the wealth and strength we might otherwise reasonably expect by the middle of the present century. The rôle of the local bodies should be that of primary school administration, and the executive work of compulsion should be under the charge of State officials, such as the district officers. Nor must there be compulsion for boys only, which would tend to still further and artificially handicap the position of Indian women. It is a matter for satisfaction that the first compulsion Act, that of Bombay, makes no differentiation. I cannot too strongly emphasise the importance of *pari passu* application of the compulsory principle to both sexes. In those instances where there are practical difficulties so great as to make a general application of compulsion impossible for the time being, there should be a fair basis of apportionment between schools for boys and for girls. The facilities for the latter should be equalised with those for the former, and the progress toward general education should everywhere be based on the equitable principle of not permitting the enormous disparity between the literacy of the two sexes to continue.

There is no running away from this need for educational diffusion, since it is a question of life and death for India. No compromise as to providing this essential groundwork of national development can be tolerated. I am well aware that the problem is largely one of finance; but care must be taken not to allow an undue proportion of the funds made available to be swallowed up in bricks and mortar. Indian opinion is strong in the view that, having regard to the urgency of the need for educational diffusion, we must not, in these early stages, allow the construction of school houses to delay the more vital work of teaching. There are evidences that this view is also held by thoughtful English educationists in India.[1] Teaching, as the Buddha and other great lights in the religious evolution of India personally demonstrated, can be carried on by men with a sense of vocation in the humblest places and under apparently untoward conditions. The greatest teachers

[1] "The modern tendency in India to extravagance in bricks and mortar for schools and colleges should be checked. Many experienced observers believe that far less expensive buildings than those at present erected are adequate for Indian educational purposes. . . . It is for the State to put money into the making of men far more than into ornate buildings. In particular the national [primary] schools should be of the simplest construction."—The *Times* Educational Supplement, Indian article, 29th November, 1917.

of ancient India were forest dwellers and gathered their students round them in the open air. A slowing of the pace in order to wait for good buildings and other conditions of an ideal state of things would be a crime against the young life of India and her future generations.

CHAPTER XXIII

HIGHER EDUCATION

THE legitimate boundaries of primary instruction have to be determined in laying down any sound programme of secondary teaching. This important point should be settled by each province state according to its conditions, needs, and means. The secondary and technical schools should be of the nature of a voluntary superstructure on the foundations of the primary and obligatory courses. The question of early technical and scientific instruction for those who do not contemplate the advanced teaching that can only be obtained from university work should be considered when the average secondary "gymnasia" are formed. An indirect but clear aim of the teachers should be to give the boys and girls such interest in their work as to make it an individual ambition and desire to become undergraduates for the purpose of pursuing the higher branches of special training. Thus economical reasons would operate as to the extent of individual study, and promising students who could possibly afford it would continue their training as undergraduates for their own benefit and that of the nation.

Under a system of general elementary compulsion we shall soon be faced with the question whether there is to be what is known as co-education in all the secondary institutions. The ideal solution will be for parents to have the option of sending their daughters to the secondary institutions open to all, but at the same time to provide sufficient special institutions for girls to develop and meet the national requirements for the education of women on lines which take account of Indian traditions and standards. Each province state would be required to make provision, according to the standard of local needs and means, for sufficient secondary education both to provide workers of every kind in the middle walks of life, and to make the road to higher knowledge broad enough for everyone with the means and aptitudes to reach the university. These are the ideals of the secondary institutions of the United Kingdom, where only a very small proportion of pupils proceed to the university or even attempt to matriculate.

In the realms of higher education, the system initiated sixty years ago and only now being modified by new foundations, of setting up a very few central examining universities, affiliating colleges over immense areas, has proved unwieldy and mechanical. It is unknown in other parts of the world, and is too soulless to be a living, energising method of building up the intellectual and moral life of the nation. Since these great universities have grown with the modern history of India, I do not favour their abolition. They should remain and be given a reasonable extent of federal jurisdiction and power. But, side by side with them, we need not one or two merely, but thirty or forty residential teaching universities, as well as examples of the continental type of lecturing and free universities. We must have no rigid, cast-iron system of universal application. As Lord Hardinge's Government declared five years ago, only by experiment will it be found out what types of universities are best suited to the different parts of India.

It is for her to profit by the accumulated experience of more-advanced countries, bringing into her service, side by side and in many places, the varying methods by which society has so far endeavoured to provide the higher culture. For instance, in a country like India, where many men after reaching a mature age and winning a reasonable degree of financial independence show a commendable thirst for knowledge, there is much to be said for the provision of a few universities on the model of the excellent institutions of Switzerland, providing for every age and class, at moderate fees, regular lectures and courses in different fields of study, and granting degrees according to the creative work of the individual. It is not for so vast a country to take one European or American example for slavish imitation, but to bring into her service all the best-known forms and types, in order to provide scope for developing particular capacity.

Here, again, as in all other branches of the educational problem, the financial issue is important. One advantage of universities open to all ages, as in Switzerland and France, is that many well-to-do people will attend the courses, and that some at least of those who benefit by its teaching will be moved to render substantial financial help. More and more, as time goes on, will wealthy citizens be impelled by the earnest educational spirit abroad to give of their abundance, and those of moderate means of their sufficiency, to the cause of education in all the variety of its needs. But private munificence cannot take the place in educational provision which rightly falls to the community as a whole. It is for each province state to shoulder the main responsibility for the attainment of the ideal set forth in the gracious words of the King-Emperor, in replying to the address of the Calcutta University in January, 1912. The ideal is that of a network of schools and colleges so that, in the words of His Majesty, "the homes of my Indian subjects may be brightened and their labour sweetened by the spread of knowledge with all that follows in its train, a higher level of thought, of comfort, and of health." Just as certain generations in Europe, namely, those of 1790 to 1815, and of the present day, have been called upon to bear the immense sacrifice of guarding the future of their countries from foreign aggression and military subjection, so the present generation in India must make greater sacrifices than would have been requisite but for past neglect, to deliver her from the grip of ignorance, poverty, and disease.

Closely associated with this beneficent campaign is the difficult and passion-raising question of media of instruction. In many quarters English is regarded as the fitting all-prevailing *lingua franca* of higher education. This feeling found strong expression in the Imperial Legislature some three years ago, when an unsuccessful motion in favour of greater resort to the vernacular media in secondary schools drew from Mr. Surendranath Bannerjee the declaration that any proposal involving a curtailment—even a possible curtailment—of the area of English instruction would be viewed in Bengal with misgiving, and even with alarm. Yet there are vast numbers, especially in Northern India, who would like Hindi to become not only the *lingua franca* of higher instruction, but the national language and tongue of the whole country. Others, especially among the Mahomedans, have similar dreams respecting Urdu, the other great branch of Hindostani. But I believe the great majority of instructed Indians regard with considerable apprehension these passionate disputes about the vernaculars, an unhappy feature of modern life borrowed from European racial and linguistic quarrels in "ramshackle empires" (to use Mr. Lloyd George's phrase), such as Austria-Hungary, Russia, and Turkey.

Patriotic instincts should lead Indian thinkers and statesmen to resist the desire of one part of Upper India to impose its language, Hindi, on the rest of the peninsula. We saw in an earlier chapter that it was the centralising policy of the North that broke up the Mogul Empire. It is curious that even now, in the provinces where that Empire set up its successive capitals, there is a marked tendency to claim to be "the real India," and to look upon the great provinces of the South and East as mere addenda. The carrying out of any such spirit in the linguistic field would strike a fatal blow at the successful establishment of the great, federated, vital, unmechanical India of to-morrow.

If it be maintained that differences of languages will weaken the national unity, we may adduce by way of disproof the example of the Swiss Confederation. This well-knit political unity, as strong and real as any to be found, and covering a tiny area in comparison with India, has three essentially different languages, French, German, and Italian, and innumerable patois of each of them are spoken. The United States of America have been frequently quoted as an ideal for Indian federation, and yet more newspapers and books in different languages are produced in the vast Republic than in the whole of Europe put together. To force the beautiful Bengali language, with its rich and growing literature, the mother tongue of Rabrindranath Tagore, to give up its national position in this day of its development would be a crime against culture and civilisation. Mahrati, Gujarati, Tamil, and Telugu have still to develop their literary possibilities. But philological history gives us many examples of a language, after centuries of oral use by large numbers, taking on a literary character and breaking out like water cutting a channel down the rocks. Thus Italian lived a subterranean life for centuries until the imaginative genius of Dante forced recognition from the world. We may confidently anticipate that the great languages of Southern India, under the quickening impulse of the Renaissance, will reach literary maturity, and each make its characteristic contribution to the wealth of human culture and civilisation.

Again, it would be an act of cruel vandalism to deprive the Indian Mahomedan of Urdu. Nor would the deprivation be merely sectional, for it is spoken and written by large numbers of people of other faiths, and in origin it is very much more the work of cultured Hindus, well versed in Persian and Arabic, than of Mahomedans. Gifted Hindu writers of Urdu have contributed from the first to this day to its poetic and prose literature, as is clearly shown in Sir George Grierson's monumental *Linguistic Survey*,[1] and it would be a calamity, through a narrow and shortsighted particularism, to deprive large numbers of Hindus from the pleasure and instruction they derive from a language that has intimate relations with the classical tongues of Western Asia. For the humanistic culture of India, as for her political development, we must have as broad a basis as possible: ordered variety instead of a mere mechanical similarity.

Let all the main Indian languages and their literary potentialities receive the fullest encouragement, with universities devoted to them when possible. The fact that the differences between the main groups, if we except the Dravidian South, are not cardinal, such as between, say, Finnish or Magyar, or French and Dutch, should in the long run lead to each gaining strength from the development of the other. Philological science long ago taught us that languages are the natural expression of a people's inner life and mentality. To artificially force some to adopt the idioms of others is nothing but a cruel injustice only appropriate to the ideals of Prussian kultur. Pragmatism and vital character and quality are the essential needs —not imitation of some external ideal of unity which, when artificially propped up, say by the Tsars from Peter the Great to Nicholas II, leads to the greatest disasters and divisions. The India hoped for in this book is one in which the love of a common Motherland will be expressed and exercised in every form and language. It seems

[1] Vol. IX: Indo-Aryan Family, Central Group; Part I: Western Hindi and Panjabi. Calcutta. Govt. Press. 1916.

to me a wise decision on the part of His Exalted Highness the Nizam to make Urdu the language of the Osmania University he is establishing, but with English a compulsory subject.

Still, as I have sought to define, not a Utopian and perfect India of the far-off future, but an India that can and ought to be shaped for the morrow of peace, it has to be regretfully recognised that as things are it is not practicable, except in the singular situation of the premier State, to set up the main universities with any other language than English as the medium of instruction. To translate the wide range of text-books and other literature necessary for an adequately equipped university must be a costly and in many respects difficult task, and unless backed up by the power of a mighty prince such as the Nizam, is liable to break down in the present stage of literary development of the Indian vernaculars.[1] The task of the day is to concentrate on the creation of varied universities teaching in English, some based on the residential system; others open to matriculated students from affiliated colleges and examining for degrees; and others, on the Swiss model, open to all and bestowing their honours according to the creative work brought before the university authorities, without investigation of the general qualifications of the writers.

Under such varied systems, the problem of the higher education of women would be less difficult than that of primary and secondary instruction. In the case of the non-residential examining colleges,

[1] I do not forget that after modern universities were established in Russia and Japan, they had to depend upon translations for decades, and the native language developed naturally with time.

the women can be enrolled at affiliated institutions. Where the Oxford and Cambridge model is followed, it will be necessary to start special residential colleges for them. Universities of the third category on the Swiss model, as in Paris and Lausanne, will be equally open, regardless of sex, for lecture courses, a small payment being made for each course.

Science and natural philosophy must play a leading part in the curriculum of each kind of university that has been advocated. There must also be higher scientific and research institutions all over the country. The Indian Institute of Science at Bangalore, initiated by Jamsetjee Tata, and Sir Jagadis Chunder Bose's Research Institute in Calcutta—inspired by a noble ideal of pure scholarship—these are models which should be followed on a large scale both in the provinces and principalities. Special institutions are also needed for the study of higher geology and mineralogy, and also for medical and pathological research, with which I deal in the following chapter. The broad aim must be to make India sufficiently well equipped educationally to give her sons the general and special culture they seek, so that the ambitious should no longer be under the virtual compulsion to spend years of their normal student life abroad.

CHAPTER XXIV

PUBLIC HEALTH

A SHORT time before Gokhale's lamented death, he and I spent an afternoon in calling from the depths of Valhalla great men of every kind distinguished for the beneficence of their individual contribution to human amelioration and progress, and tried to imagine how and to what extent they could have served India in our generation. The list was long and varied, and, so far as I can remember, began in the mists of quasi-mythological times and ended with men of our own day who shall be nameless. When the long review was over Gokhale said, "Well, it's Ling that India needs most."

Those who do not know the physical disabilities of modern India may be surprised at this choice of a saviour of society by so keen a politician as Gokhale. Yet, when we remember what were the actual conditions of health in Scandinavia in the past and what they are to-day, we have to admit that the great work done by Ling, and carried on after his death by the elder Branting,[1] has revolutionised for the better the conditions of human life over a large area, and set an example followed by other countries to an extent for which there are few parallels in the history of mankind. Though

[1] Father of the well-known international Socialist leader M. Branting.

it is doubtful if the whole mass of the Scandinavian peoples outside Ling's native Sweden has followed his teaching, we know that it is carried out on a considerable scale in Denmark, Norway, and Finland, and that the indirect influence of his work has been strongly felt in other parts of the European Continent. In Germany and Austria the physical drill imposed under the compulsory military system is largely based on the classical exercises invented by Ling. Until his influence was felt at the beginning of the nineteenth century, tuberculosis and many other diseases due to sedentary degeneration of the human body, were common in Sweden and throughout Northern Europe. The average duration of life was short, and so weak were the inhabitants, except in the military forces, that foreign observers invariably began their descriptions of the country with pitying allusions to this characteristic. To-day it is doubtful if we can find in any society quite such a large proportion of physically strong and healthy beings as amongst the countrymen of Ling.

To realise the significance of Gokhale's selection, the actual physical condition not only of the masses, but of the upper, middle and educated and urban classes in India to-day has to be considered. Diabetes, the disease which carried Gokhale himself away in what should have been the high-tide vigour of middle age, is a special plague of the upper and middle classes of our country. It is common from early manhood in the wealthy and commercial classes, also students and teachers, reducing the average of life amongst them to an extent which, if generally recognised, would bring to India, in her struggle against this tenacious enemy, the sympathy and assistance of the civilised world. The same upper classes, especially the women, suffer terribly from preventible tuberculosis.

A heavy handicap is placed upon national progress by the cost to India of losing a considerable proportion of her best sons from diabetes or tuberculosis soon after they have reached full development. To illustrate from only one province, and names that at once spring to the mind, Telang died at forty-three and Gokhale at forty-nine. Taking one particular community in the province with which I am directly connected, such men as Jairaz Peerbhoy and A. M. Dharmsey, who gave promise of going a long way in the service of their country, died young from diabetes. Similar examples could be given by the score from every part of India. It is scarcely too much to say that this disease lays a paralysing hand on a large proportion of the best intellects of India before the meridian of life is reached.

Had India been granted a national Ling the immense importance of physical activity in fresh air would have been known to all classes. This has still to be understood and appreciated. It is no exaggeration to say that, except for a few of our younger princes who derive full benefit from riding and polo, the school-going upper and middle class population is much underworked physically. One of the greatest regrets of my life is that during those all-important years, fourteen to twenty-one, there was no Swedish teacher in Bombay to make me go through half an hour of scientific gymnastics each day. Had such a facility been within my reach, how infinitely greater would have been my capacity for public service! The occasional cricket, football, or hockey played by a small minority of students can never replace as a national means of physical culture the daily and regular practice of a system such as Ling's, designed to make every muscle and nerve of the human body fit for its proper function.

Every great national advance, however beneficial, brings with it some drawback or disadvantage. Thus the promotion of education on Western standards imposes a school life which is not natural and native to the soil. One disadvantageous result is that such excellent national pastimes as wrestling and the use of clubs (to which India has given her name) have tended to die out, or become a mere means of livelihood or of prize exhibitions on the part of a few professional strong men. But such drawbacks can be provided against. Educational diffusion in India should be accompanied by general physical drill, under the instruction of teachers trained on scientific principles derived from the original discoveries of Ling. Girls as well as boys must be subjected to suitable drill, for otherwise we shall be building on foundations of sand. With the love of fresh air instilled in school girls as well as boys, a life of seclusion behind the purdah, that potent cause of the scourge of tuberculosis amongst our women, will cease to be widespread in the classes by whom it is now followed. A girl brought up in a healthy school, with fresh air and full exercises and instruction in the use of a sensible toilet, will no more accept the life of immurement in the dark, musty rooms of the zenana than she will go to suttee of her own free will.

By an irony of social conditions, while the upper,

middle, and urban classes generally suffer from inadequate physical activity, fully comparable havoc has been wrought among the rural masses by the excessive physical toil and under-nourishment described in the chapter on agriculture. Here it need only be said that the Indian peasant, whether man or woman, is little more than a skeleton. The body has a framework of small bones covered by skin burned in early childhood by undue exposure to heat and cold in laborious field work. At forty, if the woman lives so long, she is old and broken; and before reaching that age the men, though they go on working in the fields till death, are worn and shrivelled. Physical exertion, which would be excellent if not begun prematurely and if sustained by sufficient nourishment, has robbed them of their vitality as thoroughly as the most bitter misanthrope could desire.

So far we have been dealing with what may be described as average conditions. But the sad picture would be very incomplete without the inclusion of reference to the widespread ravages of malaria, and the frequent recurrence in different parts of the country of epidemics of plague, cholera or small-pox, every few years. When such visitations come the poverty-stricken Indian, unable to go well shod or to sleep on a cot, has his body both when waking and sleeping in direct contact with the ground habitat of the rats and fleas that propagate the disease. Again, the average working man, sustaining life on a few grain foods, is exposed to constant internal derangement, making him susceptible to cholera. Need we wonder that though twenty-two years have passed since plague began its ravages in India on a considerable scale, it has still to be eradicated? Recently the chief medical journal of Great Britain stated that the disease has carried off nearly 10,000,000 victims, and that the time has not yet come for science to claim to have gained a decisive victory.[1]

Malaria is endemic over a very large part of the country. It does not kill with the quick relief of plague or cholera, but to the average peasant it means an existence of long-drawn misery to end with death. The annual average fever mortality in the last census period, in the United Provinces, was 27·8 males and 28·3 females per mille, and in Bengal the corresponding figures were 24 and 23 per mille. The Bengal Census Report for 1911 puts the case effectively when it observes: "Not only does it [malaria] diminish the population by death, but it reduces the vitality of the survivors, saps their vigour and fecundity, and either interrupts the even tenor or hinders the development of commerce and industry. A leading cause of poverty and of many other disagreeables in a great part of Bengal is the prevalence of malaria. For the

[1] "Owing to the fluctuations of the mortality and the temporary reduction at times in the number of plague deaths, some sanguine minds have confidently predicted a speedy cessation of the epidemic, on the score that its virulence was becoming exhausted, and that, in popular language, 'it was burning itself out.' The highest point of plague prevalence was reached in 1907, when no fewer than 1,315,892 persons died of the disease during the year. The next two years witnessed a considerable decrease in plague mortality, for in 1908 only 156,480 and in 1909 178,808 deaths were recorded. Unfortunately, this diminution has not been maintained, and for the last eight years the annual average number of plague deaths has been 420,836. The latest figures available —namely, the provisional returns for 1917—show that close upon half a million of lives were sacrificed in India to plague during the year. So that it cannot be said that, taking India as a whole, there are as yet any indications that the pestilence is abated."—The *Lancet*, 23rd March, 1918.

physical explanation of the Bengali lack of energy malaria would count high." This state of affairs has greatly impressed itself upon my friend Lord Ronaldshay during his first year as Governor of Bengal, and I note with gratification that he has instituted a vigorous anti-malarial campaign, and has called for the co-operation of the educated classes. In a recent speech he pointed out the serious economic evils of the general prevalence of a disease estimated to be responsible for 200,000,000 days of sickness in the presidency every year, and causing the death of from 350,000 to 400,000 annually.

Some loathsome forms of disease, such as leprosy and elephantiasis, and the extreme forms of eczema, are to be found more often in India than in any other country under enlightened rule. There is only one of the great and baffling ills found in most countries which is rare; and that is cancer. The explanation is that the disease does not usually manifest itself until after the forties. In India relatively few pass beyond those years. Though it is officially admitted that the age tables of the census are unreliable, since there is a tendency for persons of maturity to greatly overstate their age, the proportion of persons over sixty to every hundred between fifteen and forty is only twelve males and fourteen females.[1]

The picture I have drawn is dark, but in no sense exaggerated. The sons of India must search with heart and soul for remedies for these calamities if their country is not to become a byword of the nations for low vitality and dangerous disease. The task is enormous and complex, but it must be

[1] Census of India 1911. General Report, chapter v.

faced. I have shown how great a contribution can be made to it by compulsory education, coupled with scientific drill and movements necessary for exercising the vital organs. Diabetes and the many other diseases due to a sedentary life will be radically checked when the urban population as a whole has learnt from early education to give a minimum of half an hour every day to the service of the body. It is the early years which decide the vigour and fitness or the inefficiency of the physical organism. The unseen organs will most benefit and develop by the habit of exercises becoming general. Games, though valuable in their place, do not completely meet the need, for they could never become daily and regular. Even the best of them, such as football and hockey, have a tendency to develop only a limited part of the physical equipment, whereas scientific gymnastics give each group of muscles beneficial play.

The great scourges of the country must be taken in hand scientifically. Such a campaign as Lord Ronaldshay has initiated should be general and determined. The sanitation of rural areas, so notoriously inadequate as to touch only the fringe of this pressing need, must be taken seriously in hand by each province state and principality. The researches of Ross have proved that with proper energy and attention malaria as an endemic disease may be stamped out. It will be an immense work; but malaria is an immense curse. Such efforts have been successful on the part of the Americans in the tropical regions of the Panama Canal, and, on a small scale and in particular areas, in the best States of South America; also in particular localities in the Dutch Colonies. In India the work must be taken in hand on a great national scale commensurate with its vital importance.

Cholera needs a sanitary and medical service set apart for the purpose of dealing with it directly any locality is threatened. Such a service must not be limited to a mere handful of men located in a provincial capital, but must be an active mobile force, always on the look-out for the prevention of the scourge. The same holds good of plague, and scientific measures of prevention and for dealing with the pests that propagate the disease must be carried out on a larger scale than hitherto. Inoculation against plague, improved and developed, ought to be as general, wherever there are signs of nascence, as the use of quinine in the malarious areas.

The worst form of venereal disease is endemic over a great portion of the Indian community. Indeed it has become so prevalent that the public is misled as to its dangers. Here, again, the researches of Ehrlich and others have brought new preventive and curative methods within reach. There should be some Indian counterpart to the various measures taken in the United Kingdom to combat the peril, as a result of the recommendations of the Royal Commission presided over by Lord Sydenham which reported in 1916. In every district there should be a peripatetic medical officer, offering advice and relief and when necessary sending sufferers to institutions provided with the equipment for the new surgical treatment.

With other loathsome diseases for long thought to be incurable, and notably leprosy, Rogers has shown what can be done by one man in face of overwhelming difficulties. But genius is rare; a

Ross or a Rogers cannot be provided to order. Investigation and experiment, however, can be carried on by the patient student of men of ordinary abilities. No country in the world offers so wide and varied a field as India for research work against human and animal diseases. As Mr. Austen Chamberlain observed, when Secretary of State for India, at the reading of a paper by the late Surgeon-General Sir Pardey Lukis, "Whether one looked at the problem in the light of the vast mass of humanity whose interests were at stake, or whether one looked at it in the light of the numberless problems which were still unsolved and which awaited the willing worker, India offered a splendid field for research and for the service of mankind."[1] The existing research institutes at Parel, a Bombay suburb, Kasauli, and Madras, and the Pasteur institutes at Kasauli, Coonoor and Rangoon, and the schools of tropical medicine at Calcutta and Bombay, are so many beacon lights showing the way towards full accomplishment of this beneficent task. Institutions with complete appliances, with a regular research staff working in co-operation with the practising members of the medical profession, should become as common as they are rare to-day. Only by multiplying them will pace be kept with the many problems still awaiting solution, or will the fruits of the discoveries be brought within the range of the labouring classes throughout the country.

All these necessities for combating the low state of Indian vitality will be costly, and the way to their full provision is along the path of political reform. There must be united and strenuous effort,

[1] *Journal of the Royal Society of Arts*, April 13, 1917.

financial and voluntary service on a scale not to be expected from a country in which the general populace, ruled by a just but irresponsible and externally recruited bureaucracy, has little occasion to learn the need for common sacrifice and the high privilege of the exercise of personal responsibility for promoting the good of the commonwealth. Only when the Government can discuss the situation with representatives of the various classes of the people, and not merely of a few privileged orders, meeting their demands for ameliorative and preventive measures with claims for the sacrifices necessary thereto, will India be able to achieve the heights of heroic devotion of men and means to the public health without which she is doomed to remain, in the realm of social efficiency, one of the most backward of the great countries of the world.

CHAPTER XXV

THE DEPRESSED CLASSES

THERE is close relation between the low standards of public health discussed in the last chapter and the moral and material degradation of the depressed classes. Our natural sympathy with the work of amelioration, and our dissatisfaction that fully one-sixth of the people should be segregated and artificially kept out of the main streams of national life, must not lead us to parrot-like repetition of the familiar assertion that the prejudices and sense of superiority of the higher castes is the all-embracing cause of the misery and degradation of the masses. In every part of the world we find a "submerged" class. In India so widespread is the poverty of the people that, judged by Western standards, an overwhelming majority, and not the outcastes alone, can be described as depressed or submerged. Long familiarity with this all-pervading poverty, however, leads to the application of these terms on the basis not of poverty, but of membership of the "untouchable" communities. Henceforth, if the task of national improvement and consolidation is to be taken in hand, we must give a wider meaning to the description of "depressed" than that of the mere position of a number of inferior sections in relation to the Hindu caste system.

A mere hypothesis will make this point clear. We will assume that a great and sudden movement toward social justice led all the Brahman and other castes of Hindu society to receive the outcastes as brothers in faith, and to accept their companionship at gala dinners throughout the land. What would be the position of these unfortunate people on the following day ? No doubt the mere fact of acceptance as the social and spiritual equals of high-caste men would bring a sense of exaltation, and there would be a general widening of national sympathy. Yet in the absence of far-reaching economic improvement, the actual position and standard of life of these unfortunate classes would remain very much what it is at present. The general mass would not be better off, though here and there the door of opportunity to rise might be opened, as, for instance, in the occasional marriage of girls to men of the higher castes.

Even to-day the generalisation that an outcaste cannot escape from his " birth's invidious bar " requires qualification. Whatever the legal disabilities of the depressed classes may have been when India was a purely Hindu society, for centuries past the power of strictly legal prevention of obtaining a better social position has been enforceable in restricted areas only. Historical instances of the rise of men of lowly origin to power and affluence abound. There is every reason to believe that if under a Lodi, a Babar, an Akbar, or a Shah Jehan, a sweeper raised himself, through superior merit, to wealth and influence, the State would not have allowed the caste hierarchy to drag him down to his former status. The

Brahmans would not have had social relations with him; but such a successful ex-sweeper would certainly come into business contact with his Brahman neighbours, to their material benefit, from time to time. For more than a century and a half the supreme power in India has been exercised by a nation which bases its code of justice on the equality of all men in the eye of the law. In certain provinces or states, and at certain periods of reaction, even within this period, the power of society under hierarchical influence has been exerted to press back some ambitious members of the untouchable classes. But it cannot be seriously maintained that in any British province a sweeper can be restrained from rising to affluence and social position if favourable opportunity is allied to exceptional abilities. The open competitive examination for the Indian Civil Service, and many other tests on a similar basis, know no distinction of caste or creed.

If the artificial restraint has been so small why, it may be asked, are there not more cases of "untouchables" rising to positions of wealth and trust? The answer is that in a country without compulsory education, and without a form of government giving all classes the subconscious self-respect afforded by the possession of a recognised voice in affairs, social injustice is inevitable. Superstition reigns and the material framework of society is such that it is ordinarily impossible for those who are lowest economically to improve their position, except in such a minor degree as to make the amelioration scarcely perceptible. Nor can the depression be attributed entirely to the pressure of the religious and social system under

Brahman domination; for it is not to be forgotten that there are many families belonging to the higher castes, sometimes even Brahmans, whose average condition of life is no better than that of the hereditary unfortunates.

It is well known that many members of the depressed classes improve their socio-economic position by embracing Christianity. What does the missionary do to and for the convert besides baptising him? Very often he is taught to read and write not only the vernaculars, but English. From childhood in Christian families cleanliness and the general laws of health are impressed on him and his. A boy of aptitude is placed in the way of learning, and he may rise, not only to teaching and preaching, but to other learned professions. When such advantages are within reach of each "untouchable" family, economic forces will operate so to raise the backward communities, that, in spite of the prejudices of Brahman orthodoxy, the social position of many of its members will approximate to the level of that of the highest castes. The Brahman could still object, on caste grounds, to intermarriage or intimate social relations with a successful Pariah. Though a religious basis is claimed, the exclusiveness of the Brahman mainly arises from social prejudice. Until within recent years the same attitude of mind was common in Europe. Two or three generations ago a successful Jew was as much an object of aversion on the part of the average country squire in England as a successful Sudra is to the Brahman. In Germany to this day Jews and certain urban classes are looked upon with undisguised social prejudice by the rural gentry. If the economic position of the "untouchable" in India is raised and educational diffusion gives him equality of opportunity with his neighbours, caste prejudice will not be able to depress him or condemn him to treatment any worse than that which was meted to the Jew even in England within living memory.

When all is said, however, there is no running away from the seriousness and urgency of the task of economic and social amelioration. The only object of my preliminary warnings against the assumption that the mere abrogation of caste rules would effect this reformation, is to emphasise the need for dealing with the problem from every point of view. The patriot and the social reformer must not be content to run after the will-o'-the-wisp of a religious merging, instead of doing the spade work necessary for educational, economic, and social improvement. There is no single short road to that amelioration of the lot of the Pariah which is essential to the upbuilding of Indian nationhood. Concentration of effort on the removal of the more important causes of backwardness is called for, side by side with the devotion and energy of the individual to the cause of his less fortunate neighbours before we can hope to achieve marked progress.

First and foremost, because more important than any other single agency, must be the adoption of a national policy of betterment. Under the influence of the Manchester school theories of the need for strict limitation of State agency were fashionable in mid-Victorian times; in our day, and after the experience of the last four years in particular, the matter is *res judicata*. A good many years have passed by since Sir William Harcourt declared, "We are all Socialists now." The immense development of communications, the necessity for controlling the conditions of labour, the need for raising money at rates which only the credit of the State can command for the purpose not only of defence but also of reproductive public works—these and other factors attest the recognition by all advanced communities that the moral and material development of the people is one of the main duties of the State. That even amid the clash of arms a Ministry of Health is being set up in the United Kingdom is a forcible reminder that in the most advanced countries the trend of modern society is toward making health, in the widest sense of the term, whether by the study of eugenical improvements or by intensive culture of the individual, the cardinal pursuit of the commonwealth.

The province state of to-morrow, with its strong and permanent executive, under a Governor whose main business and duty will be to keep his eyes open for every possible improvement, with its large and popular assembly representing all classes and conditions of the people, must take in hand these problems of general improvement, of raising the standard of health and comfort. It has previously been shown how far free and compulsory education for all, and including physical culture, will go to make it impossible for the population of to-morrow to accept the present conditions of life of the depressed classes.

These classes must be represented in each provincial legislature. Wherever possible they should return their own representatives; where, in the earlier stages of progress, they are so backward as to make this impracticable, it will be for the Governor to nominate their leaders for the time being. When their political equality is constitutionally recognised, they will themselves gain social self-confidence, and soon by unconscious stages realise their responsibility toward and value to the commonwealth. Such measures as civil marriage bills will be required in each province. Other measures of social justice will be an indirect result of the recognition in political representation of the legitimate place in the nation of classes without whose humble toil communal life as a whole could not be maintained.

Our main reliance on State action to improve the conditions of life of all the backward elements, whether technically belonging to the depressed classes or not, must lead to no neglect of the great opportunities on every side for voluntary social service. The Christian missionaries have set an example in this respect of what can be achieved by a body of devoted men acting in concert. The Indian Christian community has been doubled in the last three decennial periods ending with the census of 1911, and now represents about 1¼ per cent of the entire population; and this is due far less to natural increase than to the constant accession to its ranks of members of the depressed classes. Further, since 1911 there has been a developing tendency to mass movements towards Christianity, one of the perplexing problems of the missionary bodies being to make due provision for the reception and education of whole villages desiring enrolment. Though there may be natural regret on the part of educated Indians that people of their own religions are absorbed by a foreign communion, there can be no denying that the social and economic improvement which the missions bring to the poorest of the poor is a great and beneficent work. It calls for Indian sympathy, and still more for Indian imitation.

In early life I thought that the noblest ideal for an Indian Mahomedan of means or influence was to work for the education of his Islamic brethren. For many years now I have held the view that a still greater and nobler work awaits the Indian Moslem. That is the organisation throughout the country—I will not say of "missions," because of the mainly proselytising associations of the word—but of mutual help associations on a national scale, for improving the condition of the depressed classes, irrespective of their religious beliefs. Everyone with influence among them should earnestly pray that the Moslems may have the grace to recognise the need for this labour of love. Since the highest recognition of brotherhood and fellow-citizenship can only come by accepting inter-marriage, at any rate in the present social conditions of India, the Mahomedans would be justified in advancing their religious views amongst those members of the backward classes who were thus brought into touch with them for the work of common regeneration.

The most fitting and important agency, however, for this beneficent task is that of the higher castes among the Hindus themselves, and this has been recognised to some extent by the work in recent years of Hindu missions, especially in Bombay, under the influence of Gokhale and Sir Narayan Chandavarkar. No statement to which the former gave expression was more pertinent to the duty he enjoined both by practice and precept than that the problem of Indian progress is, in the last resort, the problem of raising the Indian average of character and efficiency. What the Christian missionary and the Mahomedans can do on a relatively small scale, must here become the most insistent and widespread voluntary work of the most numerous portion of the nation. With high-caste Hindus, as with Mahomedans, religious propaganda, the results of which are so often embittering and narrowing, should not be the inspiring motive, but rather the giving of a helping hand to fellow countrymen in trouble whose depression is a serious handicap to the general progress of the Motherland.

If the work is to be effective, it will be necessary to recognise the claims of social equality wherever this is possible, and to remove the embargoes on intermarriage between different sections. The various voluntary organisations, which might also comprise men of other faiths, such, for instance, as the Buddhists, would work in friendly rivalry, not with the mere object of increasing their own numbers by a few thousands, but with that of bettering the social position of the most backward, with a view to realising a common progressive nationality. In the immense fields of secondary and higher education, of special scholarships, and of widening opportunity for artistic and spiritual cultivation, and of facilitating inter-marriage between the different classes—these and other ameliorative agencies will give wide scope for the voluntary energy and patriotism of Hindu, Mahomedan, and Christian alike, when the State fulfils the primary duties of universal elementary education and of due sanitary provision.

CHAPTER XXVI

THE STATUS OF WOMEN

THE social reformation considered in the last four chapters depends in large measure on the recognition afforded to the rights and status of the female half of the population. The Prophet of Islam (who has been so cruelly libelled in the Western world, by ignorance or malice) was wont to say that men can but follow in the footsteps of their mothers towards Paradise. And it was not for nothing, according to Moslem belief, that his first convert was a woman. The word "harem," often held by the uninformed to signify a prison, or something worse, means in reality "the sacred presence," and is derived from the same root as the word used for the Holy Places of Mecca and Medina. In the ancient epics and thought of the Hindus, too, there are to be found correspondences with the veneration enjoined by Islam toward women. The Hindu ideal of womanhood has been that of a necessary counterpart without whom a man himself cannot obtain salvation.

When we consider the scientific and natural importance of woman to society, we find that numerically they fall somewhat below the male population. In India as a whole at the last census the proportion of females per thousand males in the actual population was 954. In Western Europe, on the other hand, the number of females per thousand males varied from 1093 in Portugal and 1068 in England and Wales, to 1013 in Belgium and 1003 in Ireland. Sir Edward Gait, the Census Commissioner, while admitting that the Western Europe proportions are exceptional, attributes this marked difference to the relatively high mortality amongst females in India. In natural conditions there is always a slightly greater birth of boys than of girls ; but infantile mortality being higher amongst boys, the preponderance tends to disappear. Sir Edward holds that the advantage which nature normally gives to girls in this way is neutralised by the social conditions of Indian life, and particularly by premature marriage and child-bearing, and the laborious toil in the fields of the women of the working classes.[1]

Biologically the female is more important to the race than the male. While average women are capable of earning their own livelihood like men, they are the guardians of the life of the race, and only through their natural constitution are they able to bear the double burden. Experience shows the strong probability that the active influence of women on society, under free and equal conditions, is calculated not only to bring about practical improvement in the domestic realm, but also a higher and nobler idealism into the life of the State. Those who know Moslem society from within readily admit that its higher spiritual life owes a great debt to the example and influence of women. To-day, as in the lifetime of the Prophet, probably the majority of devout and reverent followers of His teaching are women. In Christendom too the enthusiasm, idealism, and stead-

[1] Census of India, 1911. General Report, chapter vi.

fast faith of the weaker sex are of the highest value, notably in the Catholic Church. The surrender in the West of the lives of many women to piety and good works is a great antidote to the evils of general and habitual selfishness.

In relatively young countries, such as Australia, New Zealand, and some of the American States where votes have long been given to women, beneficial results have followed, and at least some of the curses of modern civilisation have been greatly mitigated. Notably the drinking saloons have been reduced in numbers and hours of trade, and have been subjected to closer supervision, while in many of the federated States they have been abolished. Even in England, where women have secured political enfranchisement only within the present year, some of the outstanding social scandals have been removed, or at least greatly mitigated, by their determined and self-sacrificing labour. In the Great War the women of the United Kingdom, France, Italy, and there is reason to believe of Germany, have eagerly devoted themselves to manifold forms of toil, at office, munition factory, and farm, and near the "front" for war purposes. They have proved themselves in patriotism and selflessness the equals of men. Refining ideas and, probably, the subconscious instinct to preserve the bearers of the race, have prevented women from actually taking the field, except in Russia, where women by their steadfastness often put to shame deserting and mutinous soldiery. But many thousands of English and French women have served the Army behind the lines, well within the danger zone; and one has only to be in London or Paris on a raid night to see the calm, heroic work performed by nurses, and the fortitude of their sisters, generally speaking.

No progressive thinker of to-day will challenge the claim that the social advancement and general well-being of communities are greatest where women are least debarred, by artificial barriers and narrow prejudice, from taking their full position as citizens. Hence it is with deep sorrow that the admission must be made that the position of Indian women is unsatisfactory, that artificial obstacles to their full service of the commonwealth are everywhere found, and that, from the point of view of health and happiness alike, women suffer needlessly through chains forged by prejudice and folly. Suttee, infant marriage, the compulsion of permanent widowhood, and the enervating restrictions of the purdah, are so many hateful caricatures of the teaching of the Prophet and indeed of the earliest and purest of the sacred writings of Hinduism, namely, respect and honour for women by protecting the persons of the bearers of the race from risks of violence. These and other social evils have so handicapped India that it is impossible to conceive of her taking a proper place in the midst of free nations until the broad principle of equality between the sexes has been generally accepted by her people.

The present abrogation of this principle is the more to be deplored since the natural intelligence and ability of Indian womanhood are by no means inferior to those of their emancipated sisters. There are abundant indications that the Indian woman, given the same chances as her more fortunate Western sisters, could contribute no less fully to the general advancement. The Dowager Lady

Dufferin wrote in her description of Viceregal life: "I have never seen women more sympathetic, more full of grace and dignity, more courteous, or more successful in the art of giving a really cordial reception to a stranger than those I met behind the purdah." We all know Indian *grandes dames*, Oriental types of such famous leaders of English society as Lady Palmerston, Sarah Lady Jersey, and Lady Waldegrave. Many of the princes owe a very great deal to the wise counsel of their mothers and wives. Amongst the commercial and trading classes, so great is the natural intelligence of many women that, in spite of the handicap of seclusion, they become real companions, helpmeets and advisers of their husbands. In a word, the natural material for feminist progress in India is good, but it is artificially kept in swaddling clothes.

The best mind and thought of the country has long seen the need for improvement in the position of women. Their emancipation has figured, from the first, in the teaching and practice of the Brahmo Samaj, and was long since effected by the small but progressive Parsee community. Social reform movements have carried on tireless crusades against the disabilities of the gentler sex, in the earlier years against vehement opposition as the late Byramji Malabari found when he was instrumental in securing legislation (1891) for raising the age of consent from ten years to twelve. To-day there is ever growing recognition of the need for educational facilities for women. Aspirations in this respect which have been stirring throughout the world are making themselves felt in India. "Thoughts have gone forth whose power can sleep no more."

Yet the change in the feminine standpoint has been coming very gradually, largely owing to a very serious mistake made by mere man at the starting-point of reform. The constant argument has been that of the necessity for providing educated and intelligent wives and daughters, sisters and mothers, for the men. This well-meaning but insolent assumption that it is for some relation, however advanced from present standards, to the other sex that women need intellectual cultivation, has inevitably tended to direct the movement into narrow and deforming channels. The time has come for a full recognition that the happiness and welfare of the women themselves, must be the end and purpose of all efforts toward improvement.

Happily, one of the great religions of the country, Islam, assures women economic independence, giving them regular and settled rights of succession to property. Under Islamic law they are not, as in England till the passing of the most far-reaching of the Married Woman's Property Acts (1882), as still in France, Italy and other parts of Catholic Europe, reduced to being after marriage and in the absence of deeds of settlement, nothing but the dependents of their husbands and to the latter having control of their pre-nuptial property. Amongst the Hindus the economic position of women is often contradictory, under interpretations of personal law governing their social customs, and differing from province to province and also as between various divisions and castes. Generally speaking the Hindu joint family system, as petrified by case-made law, operates to turn widows and married women into either domestic tyrants or slaves. It is often a question of luck in legal argument and evidence, whether or not an assertive lady of the family obtains control of the common purse, and so reduces the independence of others in the household as to render impossible a full, rich, and responsible individual life. It is to be hoped that the province states of to-morrow will be able, through their popular assemblies, to enact measures to ensure economic freedom and a reasonable uniformity of independence to Hindu women generally.

Having regard to the present constitution of Indian Government, with the absence of responsibility to the people, the reluctance of the British authorities to undertake legislation affecting the social customs of the people can be well understood. One cause of the "leave it alone" tendency is that conditions vary so greatly in different parts of the peninsula, and the work of the central Government is so absorbing that thorough consideration cannot be given to the conflicting issues which social legislation is calculated to raise. The province state, in close touch with representatives of all schools of thought, will not be so hampered. It will be in a position to further raise the age of consent, to legislate for the economic independence of women by ensuring to them the use of their own property, for giving widows and daughters the right to claim their shares and leave the joint family if so disposed. By civil marriage bills it should be made possible for natural choice in mating on both sides to extend over the whole of society. Such legal measures are essential as corollaries of voluntary social reform. Human nature being what it is, if the laws of a country are prejudicial to women, the good intentions and earnest efforts of philanthropists and reformers will not suffice to rectify the injustice done by society at large. It would be as reasonable to expect voluntary effort and goodwill to prevent robbery and theft, as to imagine that the same agencies will change for the better the condition of society, so long as the laws of the State inflict injustice on the classes to be benefited.

It is now an accepted principle of progressive rule in the West that general impartation of elementary education cannot be left entirely or even mainly to philanthropic or voluntary effort, but to be thorough and complete must be provided by the State, which is, after all, the executive arm of society as a whole. Such provision in India, as elsewhere, must be based on the principle of sex equality. This will do more good than all the speeches and crusades so long carried on for the improvement of the condition of women. In addition the various legislatures must rectify the hampering burdens imposed on Indian life by judge-made laws which have hardened what were formerly but fluid states of social economy, answering to changing conditions. The purdah system would automatically disappear if society as a whole, represented by the State, gave women education and economic freedom in their conditions of life. The reform of the laws of property should extend to women of other faiths the rights in the economic sphere which Islam bestows. It is an unfortunate fact that, through ignorance, Mahomedan ladies are not always able to assert their full rights; but this defect will be remedied by means of education.

Throughout these pages certain well-defined and by no means rare qualifications have been suggested as giving the individual the right to a direct vote for the provincial state assembly, such as a low minimum income or land tax, and moderate literacy in the vernacular. Now it is essential that the tests for enfranchisement applied to men should be extended to the other sex. If this measure of justice is not made an integral part of the widened franchise system, we may admit without further discussion that comparatively little can be expected from voluntary reform of the social position of women. If the extraneous fact that in Great Britain women suffrage has come some eighty-five years after the first great Reform Act is to be regarded as setting the pace for India, the proposed franchise measures will largely fail, for they will be founded on bad statesmanship and fundamental injustice toward one half of society. The argument that Indian reform should be on a time scale more or less corresponding with Great Britain's constitutional developments "slowly broadening down from precedent to precedent" is singularly inept, for it fails to take into account India's responsiveness to the spirit of the age. She can profit from the experience of other countries by firmly treading the roads they have made after generations of painful effort.

I have shown that Indian women are by no means wanting in natural intelligence, and with the confidence that comes of long observation, I assert that the Indian woman who has property or education manages the one and can use the other certainly as well as any man of the same social position. It would be a signal advantage to the State to have both the intuition and the naturally conservative influence of women operating in political life. Socially unjust laws would then have much shorter shrift than at present. No scheme of political reform based on the co-operation of the people with the rulers can or will succeed, if it is vitiated by the radical defect of closing the door to women on the irrational ground of sex, and not accepting equal qualifications as conferring equal rights. It may be pointed out that in India any "danger" of a substantial majority of women voters will not exist, as it would in England if absolutely equal rights had been bestowed, instead of the age of qualification for women being fixed as high as thirty. For a long time to come universal suffrage in India is out of the question, and while property and educational qualifications provide the standards the number of women enjoying the franchise will certainly be much smaller than that of men. This relative disproportion would be considerably enhanced under the proposal to enfranchise men who have rendered military service, *ipso facto.*

We must not build up the fabric of the autonomous State on weak and one-sided foundations. I am confident that an assembly to the election of which Indian women had contributed would keep nearer to the facts and needs of life, to the real and actual in the country, than one selected by men alone. I have urged that the basis of the State should be broadened in order to give the people as a whole occasion for understanding and responding to the call of sacrifice for the commonwealth. Is it to be maintained that the women of India are less capable than the men of realising the need for sacrifice ? Or are we to impose on them the acceptation of responsibility to society at large without participation in the political shaping of the State ? The progressive modernisation which depends on co-operation and understanding between the rulers and the ruled will be impossible in India unless women are permitted to play their legitimate part in the great work of national regeneration on a basis of political equality.

CHAPTER XXVII

BRITISH AND INDIAN SOCIAL RELATIONS

SINCE the status of Indian women has been a considerable factor in discussions of the question of social relations between Britons and Indians, its consideration may fitly follow the previous chapter. It is with some reluctance, however, that I take up the subject, for I have always felt that the tendency in many quarters has been to exaggerate its importance, and to overlook certain obvious considerations. I yield to no one in abhorrence of claims to superiority based on grounds of race or colour alone. I have often heard distinguished officials maintain that one of the outstanding causes of political discontent in India is the lack of good social relations between rulers and ruled. The evils of arrogant pretension in the diversified social structure of India are great; but I must confess that this aspect of the matter has been presented in exaggerated forms on both sides, and its influence for good or evil has been greatly over-rated.

The fact is that the political desires and economic necessities and ambitions of India derive their momentum from within; so that even if the social relations between "Europeans" (as they were classed before the war) and Indians had been ideally good, these political and economic aspirations still would have the same forces behind them calling for change. There is something very fanciful in the idea that mere social reunion would suffice to create a good understanding between officials and people, when we remember that the number of Indians who could come into friendly contact with higher officials on the basis of the equality which intellectual culture and other standards of life bring would be but a drop in the ocean of the Indian population. Lord Morley's repeated observation when at the India Office that bad manners, reprehensible in any part of the world, are a crime in India, is true so far as it applies to the conduct of officials in their business character and quality as administrators, in other words as public servants. But we must not go to the extreme of imagining, as some have done, that each Englishman and woman in India is an unofficial ambassador of that race to peoples of another civilisation, and that his or her manners, or want of them, constitute a burning question.

When complaint is made that certain institutions are closed to Indians on racial grounds, we must be careful not to lump together things having no real resemblance. We must distinguish between services of public utility and the action of private bodies or institutions. Nothing can be more objectionable than that the railways, now mainly State-owned, though often worked by companies, should differentiate to the extent that they do between accommodation for European and Indian intermediate and third-class passengers, or that there should be cases of gross incivility and even of ill treatment by European travellers of Indians who are seeking or have obtained accommodation in the higher classes for which they have purchased tickets. On the other hand, there is something at best childish, and at worst nauseating, in the longing shown by a few snobs to force their way into purely British clubs.

The true solution of the social problem is to leave Indians and Englishmen to form close friendships, as they have done in the past and will do in the future, when there is mutual esteem and appreciation, and to allow them to develop expressions of their sentiment according to the circumstances of the case. A Brahman, to whom the admission of beef to the cook-house would occasion intense horror, can only be expected to receive his English friends in afternoon calls, or over a chess-board, or at a bridge table. On the other hand, the Parsee naturally carries on his intercourse by an invitation to dinner or lunch. Amongst Indians themselves there are clearly marked groups accustomed to regular social intercourse, and there is nothing extraordinary or unnatural in English exiles from their own land often prefering, in brief hours of relaxation, to meet each other rather than Indians.[1]

Where tastes are common, such as the love of sports, ranging from public and popular recreations like racing and cricket, to the select and expensive sports of polo and big game shooting, the natural interests of Englishmen and Indians have long brought them together on the healthy basis of equality and emulation of sporting skill.

[1] "We must take human nature as it is, and not harshly blame the instinct which makes Englishmen, who are day by day immersed to the eyes in Indian interests and affairs, hunger for one little spot where they can, for an hour or two, entirely shut out the obsession of the Orient."—Mr. William Archer's article "Manners in India," *Fortnightly Review*, July, 1914.

In December last some 150,000 spectators witnessed the progress of the Bombay quadrangular cricket tournament, extending over eight days, between British, Hindu, Mahomedan, and Parsee teams. Mr. E. W. Ballantine tells us that in all his travels in pursuit of cricket, during which he has seen tremendous crowds and extraordinary enthusiasm, he has never watched so impressive a sight. Lord Harris, a quarter of a century ago, when he encouraged the game so much as Governor of Bombay, "sowed seeds which have brought forth wonderful fruit," including the "narrowing of prejudices which existed between one community and another."[1] Lord Willingdon, as Mr. Ballantine points out, has followed the example of Lord Harris in encouraging cricket both by example and precept. He has started a sports club which bears his name, and there is good ground to share the hopes of the founders that it may become to Western India what Ranelagh and Hurlingham are to London, what Saint-Cloud and La Boulie are to Paris.

Even social clubs on an expressly non-racial basis, such as the Calcutta Club and the Orient Club in Bombay, have done good work within the few years of their existence. Such institutions will have a great future when wealth and culture have made the average standard of comfort and rational recreation amongst Indians in society as high as amongst the Europeans there. Clubs will then arise to meet the felt want, and both races will be glad to belong to them. Something of this kind is taking place in Cairo. For many years there was social aloofness between the Egyptians and the

[1] Article in *Evening News*, 25th March, 1918.

Europeans. Then the former instituted the well-known Mohammed Ali Club. The cuisine and other amenities were so excellent that the most cultured members of the European colony were readily enrolled on its books and are among the frequenters. In the regenerated India of to-morrow, it is to be hoped that not only the present great institutions for Europeans and the present smaller clubs for Indians may co-exist, but that still finer clubs open to all generally eligible without distinction of race, will add to the amenities of life in the East.

As was hinted at the beginning of this chapter, an important phase of the social question in the quite recent past was that practically all Indian ladies, excepting among the Parsees and one or two reformed Hindu bodies, such as the Brahmo Samaj, held to the purdah system. To-day amongst the upper classes that system is fast disappearing, faster than many in England or even Englishmen in India realise. This is one of those silent and momentous social changes which come gradually at first, and are suddenly found to have gathered momentum and to be finally achieved almost in a night. The majority of upper class girls born since the dawn of the twentieth century have had an upbringing that makes it impossible for them to accept the cramping conditions of the past. Their mothers, on the other hand, were brought up under traditions that make their breaking away from purdah a practical impossibility. As the new generation replaces the old and permeates society with its influence, the break with the past will come naturally and rapidly.

The large legislative assemblies proposed in these

pages will have the great incidental advantage of bringing the leading officials as a class into touch with representatives of India drawn from every section of society. Hitherto, not the least of the misfortunes of India's narrow political life has been that only a handful of men in each province have been associated with the administration by this channel. Thus the field of acquaintanceship has been narrowed out of all relation to the varied interests and condition of the people. For many men quite as acceptable, worthy and able as those on Government House lists, no way of access has existed. The large legislative assemblies of to-morrow will open to many worthy citizens, not only opportunities for usefulness, but also social vistas now generally limited to lawyers or rich men. Again, a Royal Viceroy, holding his court not only at Imperial Delhi, but during his tours of the country at Bombay or Calcutta, Baroda or Mysore, and giving the entrée to merit irrespective of race or colour, will be a potent factor in bringing about social fusion and mutual understanding.

After all, however, the keynote to improved relations is the cultivation of real affinities. In no part of the world can we expect thorough understanding and intimacy between men of different race, unless they are drawn together by some common bond of interest such as service of the public weal, sport, literature, or art. Social union as a hot-house plant is doomed to failure; but I cherish the conviction that in the India of the near future men of both races will have occasion for strengthening their natural mutual goodwill by the means I have suggested.

CHAPTER XXVIII

EFFICIENCY AND STABILITY

HAVING completed our study of Indian conditions, internal and external, and given an outline of the political and social reforms now required, we may consider some of the arguments which are put forward by those who tell us that the welfare and contentment of the people generally are bound up with the maintenance of the ideas and principles underlying British rule in the last sixty years.

Great stress is laid by the opponents of any far-reaching change of system (apart from decentralisation to give the local Governments greater powers) on the necessity for maintaining administrative efficiency. When such efficiency is superimposed on a people from without, it does not necessarily follow that the national foundations gain in strength. Sometimes indeed this so-called efficiency has a direct ratio to the national disintegration, even when its authors and promoters belong to the nation racially but do not carry the people with them. To show this we will not go back to the past, but take examples from our own times.

Such an example is afforded by Mexico. After constant rebellions, civil wars, and revolutions, culminating in the execution of the Hapsburg Emperor Maximilian half a century ago, Mexico was a byword throughout the rest of America and

Europe for all that goes to make anarchy and chaos. Then came Porfirio Diaz, a man of undoubted though limited genius. His great powers of direction and command resulted in the formation of an outwardly efficient Government. European capital, always distrustful of political instability, now made of Mexico its pet child. Hundreds of millions were lent on almost gilt-edged security terms to the Mexican State and people. Through his long ascendency of more than a generation, President Diaz—unlike Frederick II and Bismarck, though he had taken the latter for his model—subordinated the moral and intellectual improvement of the people to material development, and forgot that the education of the mass of the people would be the best security for stability and general co-operation; that if leadership was a necessary part of good government according to his ideas of efficiency, yet explanation was a necessary part of leading. "Under federal and democratic forms, Diaz exercised a strictly centralised and personal rule."[1] His standard was one of ideal force and strength, with little surface indication, save in the few closing years, of its inherent weakness. But, as in the old Eastern autocracies and bureaucracies, the common people were neglected. On his ultimate overthrow in 1911, the naked ignorance of the masses came to the surface. Mexico to-day is a worse example of internal chaos, since wholly self-inflicted, than that of contemporary Russia. There have been constant assassinations and revolutions, and the name and life of Huerta stand out as a beacon of bad government.

[1] *Encyclopædia Britannica*, 11th edn., Vol. 18, p. 343.

To all appearance Russia, too, had a government of immense strength. Many visitors and residents there were struck by the automatic obedience of the people to the administration in general, and of the administration in the most distant parts to the central Government. Mr. William Archer, a sympathetic pre-war student of modern India, quoting the example of Mexico, has warned the people of the great peninsula of the danger of a breakdown of order and a return to anarchy. If he had brought his recently published book[1] up to date, instead of leaving it as penned before the war, he might have pointed to the condition of Russia as providing a still greater warning. But the lessons to be derived should be addressed to the bureaucracy, to the rulers of India rather than to its powerless peoples. They go to show that anarchy and the break-up of society come in those countries where the mass of the people, while brought under a superimposed efficiency, remain in ignorance and poverty. The other efficiency of the Great Elector Frederic II and Bismarck has had behind it universal discipline learnt in school and army, the spread of intelligence and science, and such long-drawn and successful battles against Nature as those which have turned the sands and swamps of Brandenburg and East Prussia into the garden of Europe. An efficiency of officials and non-indigenous in spirit, such as those of Mexico and Russia, and even if impartial, as in India, not being rooted in popular knowledge and understanding by education, is a house of cards liable to break up, either from outside pressure as in Russia, or from internal weakness as in Mexico.

[1] *India and the Future*, 1918.

After the die of war had been cast thoughtful and patriotic Indians passed some weeks in doubt and fear that can be little realised or understood by non-Indians. Their feelings were well expressed by Mr. Justice Abdur Rahim, who was in England at the time, and publicly explained "the true meaning of the enthusiastic support [from India] of which England, apparently to her surprise, has received such signal proofs." The explanation was that Indians wished to avert by all means in their power the humiliation of a change from British to German rule. "We believe," he wrote, "that by remaining within the orbit of the British Empire we shall be able sooner to realise the destiny of India than otherwise."[1] As in a flash of light educated India saw at that watershed of modern history that the future of their own country was at stake. They realised that one unfortunate battle on the sea (and the history of warfare is largely a record of victory by the smaller force), an occupation of Paris and the north of France possibly leading to that of England, at a time when the new armies of Britain existed only in the conception of their authors, would have disastrous results for India. How near the Germans were to "hacking their way through" the history of those first few weeks of the war attest.

The immediate results in India of the victory the Kaiser promised his people "before the leaves fell" in the first autumn of the war would have been most calamitous. The only powers there not submerged in the flood would have been the Native States and the religious communities of long duration, forces existing before the advent of

[1] Letter to the *Times*, 14th Sept., 1914.

British rule. The country as a whole would have been exposed, like Russia to-day, to events such as followed the break-up of the Mogul Empire. It is a curious perversion on the part of some British writers to cite the Russian collapse as a warning against substantial political advancement being granted to the people of India. On the contrary believers in progress and orderly development are convinced that the case for such advancement is strengthened by the Russian collapse. It is because we are convinced that in the absence of political reconstruction there will be, sooner or later, a break-up of the edifice raised by England in India, that we hold that immediate steps are called for to prepare the vast population of our country to understand its responsibilities and noble destiny. It is because we want the discipline of the school and army, of science and exact knowledge, that we claim a form of devolution that will give India the strength not derivable from mere mandate and bureaucracy.

A few years ago, while travelling in Russia, I met an American friend, to-day one of the leading statesmen of the Allied cause, who confided to me his firm conviction that the system of Russian government centring at the Winter Palace and the Kremlin was in the same state of decay as the Mogul Empire after Aurangzeb, and that the decadence of the Romanoffs, like that of the Moguls, would carry the world to new experiences then undreamt of. Splendid and efficient as is the fabric of British rule in India to-day, it yet resembles those of Alexander III, of Aurangzeb, and of Diaz in the ignorance and poverty of the masses. The only real danger of repetition there of such events as the disintegration of Mexico and Russia would come from permitting the present ignorance and indiscipline of the masses to continue. The certain way of once and for all securing India to progressive civilisation and order, to method and discipline, lies in setting up trusted local authorities natural to the soil, corresponding to the communal life evolved in a past millennium, and placing side by side with them the best British and Indian officials available to carry out, with the consent of the governed, those measures, from universal education to military service and political enfranchisement, which have been instrumental in the evolution of all the great law-abiding nations. It is because the best Indian thought is convinced that there is no more time to lose, that we cry for a radical change of policy and of rule, a new angle of vision, a final break with government deriving authority wholly from without, and the commencement from the lowest to the highest stage of full co-operation with the people. These are the means by which the foundations of the Empire in India will be laid deep, and not only Great Britain, but Canada, Australia, and South Africa will be strengthened by the comradeship of a renewed, self-relying, and sincerely loyal partner in the united Empire.

CHAPTER XXIX

THE LIMITS OF BRITISH TRUSTEESHIP

THERE are still many English writers, Imperialists of high ability, who argue that the people of the United Kingdom will be untrue to their trust if they permit their responsibility for the good government of India to be substantially encroached upon by the people of that country. It is claimed that since the Government of India, through the Secretary of State, is responsible to Parliament, and the House of Commons and the Ministry are responsible to the British electorate, the latter are the real rulers and owners of India. This contention does correspond to the facts of the case during the last sixty years, namely, since the transfer of the administration to the Crown.

These six decades, however, have been years of preparation and political awakening, gradual at first, but cumulative and receiving a great impetus from the changed outlook the war has brought to mankind throughout the civilised world. The people of India, through their educated leaders, are addressing a serious and reasoned appeal to their fortunate British fellow-subjects, who, in addition to control of their own political affairs, in a very real sense own the soil of India. This appeal to British democracy is based both on principles of justice and rights of self-determination for nations, and on the practical necessity for meeting the actual conditions of the country. The various schools of thought as to the details of the advances required have been seeking to influence opinion in England. If the Indian people have the political sense of which there are growing signs, they will not be content with merely sectional presentations of the case to the British electorate, should the reforms proposed by the War Cabinet prove manifestly inadequate. We should then probably see a thoroughly representative deputation, not only of well-known Congress and Moslem League politicians, but of men of distinction from every class and community, men who have held the highest appointments open to Indians, landlords and nobles who have proved their loyalty to the Emperor and to their own country and race, and representatives also of the depressed classes. Such a deputation, made up of every school of progressive political thought, would address itself directly to the great British democracy.

An important consideration is that, under the Reform Act of the present year, England has become, in fact as much as in theory, a real democracy. The ultimate power is now in the hands of many millions of men and women whose free-born outlook never has been and will not be in sympathy with arbitrary power. When the eyes of the British public are opened to the fact that it is seriously argued on its behalf that a form of political ownership is at the foundation of England's rule in India, it will recoil from responsibility for the continuance of such political subordination in a vast country of which the great bulk of the British electorate, in the nature of the case, can have little or no knowledge. The great political principle for which the British Empire, and particularly the United Kingdom, have made sacrifices in life and treasure without parallel in history for four years is, in the words of the Prime Minister, "to make the world safe for democracy." This principle carries the corollary, as Mr. Lloyd George has freely recognised, that the civilised nations should have powers of self-determination and self-development. It is such powers that the voice of India, by an overwhelming majority, will demand after the war.

I rejoice in the thought that this claim to the right of self-determination has not to be pleaded and justified before a Kaiser and Imperial Chancellor in their closet, but before the great British public—all the greater now that something like universal suffrage exists. We appeal to the nation which, through Sir Henry Campbell-Bannerman and the most democratic House of Commons hitherto elected, carried out the wisest constitutional measure so far recorded in the history of the twentieth century—the conferment of self-government on the then lately conquered Dutch of South Africa and their British former enemies of the two Boer Republics. This sagacious act rendered possible the federation of South Africa, and a real union of both races. It provided the Empire in the hour of supreme need with a Botha and a Smuts, and rendered impotent the long-continued and secret machinations of Germany in that part of the Empire. One trembles to think what might have happened in South Africa after the outbreak of war in 1914 but for the courageous and far-sighted statesmanship of Sir Henry Campbell-Bannerman's Cabinet and the Parliament of 1906.

India's want of confidence in the working of the theory that the people of England are her ultimate owners is not based on merely national pride or purely idealistic reasons. The responsibility such proprietorship connotes has been so vicariously exercised as to devolve normally upon a small circle of men, and more particularly upon a Secretary of State whose continuance in office has been dependent far less on the relative merit and advantage of his services to India than on the exigencies of party convenience, or on the verdict of the electors on subjects having no relation to India. His salary has not been placed on the British estimates, and the control of Parliament over Indian affairs has been more nominal than real.

This unreality has been evidenced by the inadequacy of the attention the House of Commons has paid, during two generations of recognised responsibility, to the many misfortunes of its distant ward. How many debates, how many critical divisions, how many proposals to share the sacrifice in the battles against cholera and malaria, plague and poverty, do the pages of Hansard record? How often, with what voices, and with what power, has the House of Commons discussed the need for overcoming mass illiteracy in India? In what general elections of Parliament have votes been affected in any appreciable degree by the terrible poverty-famines or poverty-plagues of that distant country? It is true there have been animated debates, sometimes critical for the Cabinet of the day, on Indian affairs. But for the most part they have had their significance, as in the case of the repeated controversies on the cotton duties, in the voting strength of powerful home interests antagonistic to the just claims of India, such as having her tariffs shaped in her own interests rather than those of Lancashire manufacturers. Again, while some Indian grievances, for instance the "melancholy meanness" of exacting from her in whole or part the cost of using her troops in wars not directly affecting her security, have been challenged by votes of censure from the front Opposition bench, too often such debates have been marked by the desire to secure a party triumph more than by the prickings of conscience in respect to the trusteeship. In normal conditions, particularly since the burden of Parliamentary work accumulated and the time of private members' motions has been more and more curtailed, the only Indian debate of the year of any consequence has been that connected with the nominal submission of the Indian Budget, usually many months after its proposals have taken effect. In spite of frequent protests from the few members interested in India, the discussion has been relegated to the fag end of the session, often on the last effective day when members have been hurrying out of town. The smallness of attendance on these occasions has been notorious, and in the words of the present Secretary of State, shortly before he was called to the India Office, the tone of the debates "was unreal, unsubstantial, and ineffective."[1] Even this annual review has been abandoned during the war, the last debate of the kind taking place as long ago as 1913.

The fact is that since the transfer to the Crown in 1858 there has been a decided, and in some

[1] Parliamentary Debates, House of Commons, 12th July, 1917.

respects a progressive, deterioration of the influence exerted by the British Parliament over Indian administration. Before that time, when the Charter of the East India Company was to be renewed, select committees of investigation were set up and recorded evidence in which abuses were brought to light and remedies were demanded. On the basis of the reports made the successive Charter Acts ordained reforms and modified the powers of the Company in the direction of increased Parliamentary control. An outstanding example is the great Act of 1833, the Magna Charta of India, which to a great extent, unhappily, has remained a dead letter. Thus under the old régime a distinct and direct responsibility was exercised by Parliament.

The transfer to the Crown, while bringing great advantages to India, had the unfortunate effect of whittling away this responsibility, on the one hand by centralising control in the Secretary of State and his Council, without their salaries being placed on the Parliamentary supply estimates, and, on the other hand, by bestowing a vague and general responsibility on the electorate. As was inevitable, the system has worked out in practice to neglect by the British people of their trusteeship for a vast unknown conglomeration of races of a different civilisation thousands of miles distant. Such impartial writers as the late Sir William Hunter have estimated, on the basis of statistical and other material, that at least 60,000,000 Indians, a number equal to all the white races of the Empire, can afford but a single meal a day, and suffer the pangs of inadequate nourishment from birth to death. Has this mass of poverty ever been an outstanding problem at any British general election? Has it been so much as touched upon in the electoral manifestos of party leaders, or even in the addresses of Ministers from the India Office appealing to their constituents?

No doubt till such time as India obtains the full measure of self-governing responsibility now exercised by Canada, Australia, New Zealand, and South Africa, her fate must depend, to a certain extent, on the will of the British democracy. To his honour let it be said that the average well-informed man in India is not claiming that this goal can be reached in the near future. He knows that it can only come in strength and durability as the fruit of practice and experience—possibly painful experience—in intermediary stages of political advancement and self-determination. But this is no excuse for a policy of mere negation. He is quite definite in the demand that the present system under which India remains one of the poorest and most backward countries of the world, should be replaced. He is prepared to see the vast political experience of Britain still leading the destinies of India in foreign and military affairs, in the adjustment of Imperial taxation, in the development of India's foreign trade, in her relations with the other parts of the Empire, and in assuring all classes and castes a fair share of electoral power. On the other hand, in respect to internal provincial administration, to taxation for the spread of education and the provision of sanitation, to the removal of the economic and other causes which have brought about the impoverishment both of the soil and the people—in these matters he is convinced that the best judges would be the representatives of the people themselves, and those executive officers, British and Indian, whose position is now far too aloof to make them strong national influences, but who, in hearty co-operation with the elected assemblies, will lead India along the path toward a happier future. Further, he maintains that the only sure preventative of the transferred powers falling into the hands of a caste oligarchy or a minority of the rich and educated, is to frankly accept the diversity of Indian conditions by giving all classes direct representation. The assemblies for the creation of which he pleads must be so constituted that the nation as a whole, including the women, will exert its natural and legitimate influence.

In respect to the practical results of such devolution of authority from the British electorate to the representatives of all the communities of India, there is a tragic non-comprehension on the part of some conservative elements in England. They believe that such rights would be exercised in the direction of breaking away from the British connection. It is true that (largely owing to a system which, like a load on the chest, checks or prevents even small self-willed movement) there are foolish and mad individuals who may be styled anarchists, since they regard separation from the Empire as the legitimate aim and ambition of their country. For the British electorate and Parliament to allow their generosity and sense of justice toward the vast peninsula to be consciously influenced and deflected to the smallest extent by the existence of this small body of freaks would be at once so inequitable and so wanting in the sense of proportion as to be wholly inconsistent with

British political traditions. It is difficult to believe that some of those who most magnify the importance of such passing and insignificant manifestations of a perverted spirit of anarchy could challenge this view with any strength of conviction. It is not surprising that the belief is entertained in India that they use this horrible fact simply as a handy argument and weapon to beat back her legitimate aspirations toward a worthy place within the Empire. By way of reassurance, not of exculpation, it may be recalled that every great country, except Great Britain herself and United Germany, has passed through epochs in which anarchism has shown its teeth. This was the case in France a quarter of a century or so ago, when President Carnot, perhaps the most estimable politician of the Third Republic, was assassinated at Lyons. Italy too has had her bad times, as well as Ireland and the United States. In unhealthy political conditions, like those of Russia under the Tsardom, the disease finds fertile soil and becomes endemic. But in a healthy State, where the process of amelioration is continuous, the fever is thrown off in the course of a few years.

To maintain that the system of the last sixty years must be continued in the interests of law and order is to wholly misunderstand the spirit and aspirations of enlightened Indian opinion. If such counsels are listened to and no substantial instalment of reform is proposed to Parliament, the conclusion of the war would be the signal for strenuous efforts to place the situation prominently before the British electorate, in whose sense of justice and fair play India will have staunch faith and confidence until it has been proved to her that this faith has been misplaced. Counter agitation on the part of conservative elements in England, leading to contentious argument at the hustings, is to be deprecated. Whatever the result, whichever side was vanquished, such agitation would leave bitter memories behind. The illogical framework of Indian rule and administration cannot in any case go on unaltered, having regard to the pledges of August 20, 1917. I am convinced that if a large measure of initiative is not given to India by those in authority, the British democracy, with its inherent sense of right and wrong, will see to this being done.

CHAPTER XXX

INDIA'S SHARE IN THE WAR

THOSE who argue that the position of the British electorate as the national trustee and guardian of India should be maintained as at present, overlook the consideration that one important step taken last year, while excellent in itself and thoroughly approved by Indian opinion, is entirely inconsistent with the relationship of guardian and ward. I mean Britain's acceptance of the contribution of £100,000,000 towards the cost of the war offered by the Government of India. It is true that in September, 1914, the Imperial Legislature, at non-official instance, adopted a resolution expressing a wish for the people of India to share, not only in the actual military effort, but also in "the heavy financial burden now imposed by the war on the United Kingdom." But the amount and form of the contribution made some two and a half years later was decided by executive authority without reference to the Legislature, though of course sanction was obtained, after the offer had been made and accepted, to the taxation proposals for meeting the obligation. The offer came from the Viceroy and his Executive, who are constitutionally the agents of the Secretary of State, himself dependent on the British electorate.

When Mr. Chamberlain, in meeting Lancashire opposition to the increased cotton duties for this purpose without corresponding rise in the excise on Indian cloth, argued that the gift had to be taken as it was offered without haggling. Mr. Asquith, while not supporting the Lancashire opposition, reminded the Secretary of State that the British Cabinet, through the India Office, really shared the responsibility for the decision alike in principle and detail.[1] Now a guardian has no right, whatever his own difficulties may be, to take from his ward any substantial help, however cheerfully the benevolence may be viewed. The fact that, partly to meet the new obligation, the wealthy classes in India are assessed to a higher and graded income tax and a super-tax far beyond the dreams of the late Lord Cromer and his school, shows that in practice the Government of India now go beyond the narrow line which should mark the relationship of trustee and ward.

It must not be supposed for one moment that Indian opinion, although not consulted in any recognised way beforehand, was in any sense out of sympathy with the decision. Who are the thousands of people who eagerly came forward and subscribed to the War Loan, which brought in nearly two-fifths of the total liability assumed while the Finance Member had not felt it safe to estimate a larger quota than one-tenth? Who are the people who, in a poor country where even such national institutions as the Hindu and Mahomedan universities cannot raise a crore of rupees in the course of a decade, came forward and gave that amount in a single day, on December 12

[1] "A matter of this kind is a matter that had to be considered before any final proposition was made, by friendly discussion between the Government of India and the Secretary of State."—Mr. Asquith in the House of Commons, 14th March, 1817.

last, to war charities? Who are the people that have crowded every charitable bazaar and fill every list of subscriptions for the war? The reports of such organisations as the Bombay Presidency Branch of the Imperial Indian Relief Fund show that in little hamlets to be numbered by the thousand throughout the province substantial sums have been raised. There is more starvation and grinding poverty in a typical Indian division any day of the year than there has been in Belgium during the German occupation; yet, a real beggar's mite, Indian subscriptions to Belgian relief funds have come not only from the great cities, but from the smallest provincial towns. No one can maintain that all this has been done, or could have been done, without the general support of the people.

If we look at India's contribution to man-power in the war we find that recruitment has reached dimensions such as would not have been dreamed of in days of peace. The stream has not flagged with the long continuance of the war, and it has been announced that the recruiting figures during January last, including nearly 20,000 combatants from the Punjab and the United Provinces alone, were larger than in any previous month of the protracted struggle. To these results the Indian princes have enthusiastically contributed, and some of them—the rulers of Hyderabad, Gwalior, Bikanir, Kolapore, Kapurthala, Patiala, and Jind to mention only a few—have brought recruits by the thousand. Moreover, in the later phases of the war the Indian Empire has sent out labour battalions, totalling to scores of thousands, to all the battle fronts, and particularly to France and to Mesopotamia. Had India earnestly set out years ago with favouring breezes on the voyage to greater political liberty and the extension of economic prosperity for the masses, the contribution, actual and potential, to the man-power of the war would have been enormously greater. You cannot make the average landless labourer, who has starved since childhood, and is little more than skin and bones, fit to go to war or to carry arms. Should recruiting officers be so ignorant of their work as to accept such a man, his wretched physique would expose him to disease and render him utterly unfitted to cope with the fatigues and hardships of campaigning.

Much has been made in quarters unsympathetic to India's legitimate aspirations within the Empire of the small numbers of Indians joining the Indian Defence Force under the measure passed in the spring of 1917, open only to the classes from which the Indian Army is not ordinarily recruited. Here it must be remembered that there was considerable dissatisfaction with the decision that these territorial forces could not be officered by Indians. The training was to be under the command of selected British officers, and the only indication the official communication gave of any possibility of advancement was that the soldiers of the force, when qualified, would be eligible for promotion, and a non-commissioned officer showing special qualifications would be eligible for further advancement, i.e. to the subordinate commissions to which Indians were restricted on racial grounds up to, and a few months after, that time. It is not to be wondered at that Indians, who had urged for fully a quarter of a century before the war the removal of the bar to their countrymen reaching the higher commissioned ranks should have felt no more than a pained and lukewarm sympathy with the movement. The fact that the numbers of the six territorial units were to be limited to 1000 each, officially attributed to "the exigencies of the war," was regarded by the organs of public opinion as indicating that Government did not want a great national force, but, on applying compulsion to European residents, were impelled to make a slight sentimental concession to the Indians who had asked to be enrolled as volunteers. There is an excessiveness of caution which takes away with one hand what is professedly given with the other, without the openness and manliness of a direct negative. A double company of Bengalis was voluntarily raised as a combatant unit under special authority granted in response to the insistent wishes of the people of the province. Its success is generally admitted. The recruits came from a better class of society than those who ordinarily accept the conditions of service in the regular Indian Army. Many of these Bengalis must have felt the injustice of a system which, from the start, barred their way to higher commissioned ranks, and their enlistment illustrates the inborn loyalty of their race and class to the Empire.

It can at least be said that, in addition to being a most important reservoir of essential supplies for Allied armies and countries, India, to the full measure of her restricted opportunities, has shared in the travail and desolation brought to the homes of the King-Emperor's subjects throughout His far-flung dominions. Indians sleep in unknown graves, and Indian bones are exposed to the wind and rain in France and China, in Mesopotamia and East Africa, on hundreds of battlefields, from the great encounters of Flanders to the small skirmishes of the African jungle. Though scattered to the dust these are in the spiritual sense enduring monuments to the good faith and trustworthiness of India.

Yet there is a school of Imperialistic thought in England ready to trust Japan and accept her as a full equal, exhibiting a strange lack of confidence in the King's Indian subjects, for which there is no single justifying fact in history. Many thousands of Indians fought and died for the British Empire before the present war. We are often reminded of the Mutiny, but seldom of the fact that during that cataclysm more Indian blood was shed for the cause of the maintenance of British rule than for its overthrow. Looked at in proper perspective, and allowing for the crude conceptions and superstitions of the uneducated revolting sepoys, the Mutiny was of the nature of a civil war between two different parties of Indians, with two different ideals of government—one purely Asiatic, the other relying on the new light that had risen in the West. Such civil wars are recorded in the histories of most countries, and when the excesses of Cawnpore are insisted upon, those of Paris and Moscow, of Petrograd and Belgrade, should not be forgotten.

When the meaning of British rule in India is thoroughly explored, we are confronted by two antagonistic theories. Thus one school employs a good many windy phrases such as "taking up the white man's burden"—phrases which came into use during the period after the downfall of

Gladstone over Irish Home Rule, when Britain was most influenced by German ideas, those of Bismarck and William II, Treitschke, and Nietzsche. It consciously or unconsciously desires the perpetuation of racial supremacy in India. The rise of Japan to a position of equality with the great European Powers has but served to concentrate upon the Indian dependency these ideals of race supremacy. To this school that vast Empire at the very best, though held in trust, is a plantation from which the English owners are entitled to derive material benefit, direct and indirect, since they have provided the country with the externals of modern civilisation, with judicial systems on the basis of equality of all races before the law, and sincerely desire to assure to the people, if and when possible, a living and decent wage. The poetic significance and romance of the death of the Indian soldier in foreign climes for the Empire is not understood by this "Imperialistic" school. It entertains a subconscious feeling that the loyal Asiatic can be happy only when his racial limitations are accepted beyond discussion. It regards his loyalty as nearer that of a faithful and noble dog to a just and loving master than to that of an equal partner in sacrifice, with the same flesh and blood.

The other school, of which Elphinstone and Malcolm, Ripon, Minto, and Hardinge have been the never-to-be-forgotten representatives in successive generations, and of which Macaulay was the brilliant Parliamentary exponent and prophet, have a nobler and ultimately more beneficial idea for England in her relation to India. It is to raise the hundreds of millions of Asiatics that the will of Providence and the play of historic forces have brought within the orbit of Great Britain to a self-respecting independent position within her dominions; it is to gladly recognise that the Indian subjects of the King-Emperor are morally and physically at least the potential equals of any other Asiatic race, including the Japanese; it is to place in their hands with joy and affection the means, through education, liberty, and trust, by which they can raise their position to be comparable with that of the subjects of the Mikado.

Under this noble ideal the British Empire of the future can confer full self-government on the peoples she has trained for the responsibility, and then take back to her bosom as the greatest and best-beloved of her foster-children the free myriads of India. Happily the Imperial Crown provides the venerated centre round which the great States of the Empire can unite. Their glory and power will be enormously stronger in a free empire than in one in which the white minority would become the embarrassed jailers of the Asiatic majority. In spite of the teaching of a handful of advocates, some of them bluntly outspoken, of white ascendancy, who usurp the name of Imperialism, we Indians maintain our faith in the true and sane Imperialism of Britain's masses, and in the conscience of those aristocratic and upper middle classes which have produced the many true and far-sighted friends India has found in England. Hence we believe the meaning and ultimate goal of British rule to be the free and living union of our great peninsula, and, as we hope, of the still greater South Asiatic federation of to-morrow, with the central mother State of Great Britain and with the strong, far-spread daughter Dominions.

During his Viceroyalty Lord Curzon spoke of the ruling princes as "colleagues and partners" in the work of Empire. To-day when we are fighting for democracy, when war has brought out the real equality in heroism of our fighting men with those of other parts of the Empire, when we proudly look at our Indian peasant V.C.'s, we feel that such a limitation of Imperial partnership is far too narrow and out of keeping with British traditions. The time has come to establish a real partnership of Viceroy, Government, princes and people through federal autonomy and representative institutions including all classes of the community. Thus will there be permanent fulfilment of the King-Emperor's expectation that the War Conference, held at Delhi at the end of April, in pursuing the immediate and essential purpose in view, would "promote a spirit of unity, a concentration of purpose and activity, and a cheerful acceptance of sacrifice without which no high object, no lasting victory can be achieved."

CHAPTER XXXI

CO-ORDINATED PROGRESS

THE dark picture of social disorganisation and economic backwardness I have been compelled to draw in the course of this study may lead some readers to the enquiry whether the people of India should not concentrate their efforts on amelioration of these conditions before they press for the political advancement I have advocated. It must be admitted that such views have been held in the past by sincere Indian patriots. Some twenty years ago there were well-known thinkers in the country who looked upon the almost exclusively political programme of the National Congress as a mistake. While some of them recommended concentration of effort on industrial and commercial development, and others regarded social reform as the great object to pursue, they were united in holding that these improvements from within would provide ample scope for the efforts and ambitions of patriots for a long time to come.

It is not to be denied that the majority of the educated classes were inclined too exclusively to the political field of action; but both sides were mistaken. Universal history bears witness that no nation can develop her full strength by concentration of effort in one branch of progress, while leaving untilled the other great fields of national culture and advancement. The growing child acquires strength and adaptation to environment by the all-round exercise of bodily functions; otherwise he runs the risk of the atrophy of some organs and excessive strain on others, sure harbingers of disease. So a young nation, or one reborn, must cultivate every fruitful branch of national activity in co-ordinated effort, progressing along all lines at the same time.

A few examples from history must suffice. In the later eighties Li Hung-Chang and other Chinese statesmen possessing the confidence of the Throne, thought out a method by which they sought to acquire from Europe her defensive strength, but neither her science nor her civilisation. On the one hand, they placed orders for the most modern guns and the best ships, and selected some of their officials to study the technique of war; on the other hand, no steps were taken to raise the masses from their ignorance. The contagion of modernism in social life was carefully prevented.

The result was that in the initial stages of the Chino-Japanese war, the costly apparatus of sea-fight and battlefield provided outside the current of national life broke down hopelessly and fell into the hands of the conquerors as among the prizes of victory. Again, the Ottoman Turks, at various periods in the latter part of the nineteenth century, made serious and earnest attempts to reform some branches of the administration, while leaving others untouched. The result was one long succession of failures.

There are positive as well as negative historical illustrations. When the Arabs, after their long period of disintegration, were illuminated by the light shed by our Prophet, they promptly, and to a degree which is still one of the wonders of mankind, developed not only conquering power and science, but simultaneously enriched themselves in spiritual life, in art, poetry, and literature, and evolved higher codes of law and remarkable commercial enterprise. They became the leading nation of the world, and to-day the West owes a great debt to Saracenic culture. A study of their history during the six centuries of Arab rise and fall, shows that the activities of the nation kept pace with each other, whether in ascent or descent. The history of Prussia from early times is well worth studying from this point of view. It shows that every branch of the country's life grew in correspondence with the health and strength of the organism.

In our own lifetime, Japan and Bulgaria provide similar instances. The peoples of the Island Empire on awaking from their long sleep avoided the mistake of China in absorbing the teaching of modern civilisation in one or two branches only. Accepting the principle of co-ordination in national progress, they started on the right lines by learning all that the West could teach, and adapting the knowledge to their own environment and best traditions. In a circumscribed way and on a much smaller scale the Bulgarians took the path of co-ordinated national progress. The late Ameer Abdur Rahman showed his statesmanship by encouraging certain branches of manufacturing enterprise in his sequestered country. Presumably he would have gone further if the tribes of Afghanistan had been ready to accept the principle of search for improvement in all that concerned the life of the nation.

If peace had been broken between him and his great neighbours we may well conjecture that after a few blows from England and Russia his factories would have been destroyed, and his subjects as a whole, not having modern knowledge, would have been unable to set up other factories in out-of-the-way places.

These historical examples are a reminder that national progress cannot be compartmented at will without danger to the body politic. Gibbon, the prince of historians, pointed out that literature and art, politeness and refinement, thrive most amongst the nations that have led the world in science and bravery, in military power and civil administration. My contention is that unless a nation develops all its faculties *pari passu*, a full, rich, and independent national life is not attainable. Thus we want in India not only social and economic, but also political advancement, without which the two former cannot be brought to fruitful maturity.

Another criticism which may be brought against the reforms suggested in these pages remains to be answered. It is the reliance placed at every suggested progressive stage, social and economic as well as political, on State help. "Why cannot the Indian leaders and those they influence effect many of these changes for themselves?" is an enquiry some readers may be expected to make. The first answer is that the relations of the modern State to the social and economic organisation of society is very different to that of a century or even half a century ago. Take the case of England: can it be held that without the Compulsory Education Act of Mr. Gladstone's first Administration, the successive measures for regulating factory and other labour, compulsory vaccination, and repeated legislation to prevent the spread of infection, the efforts of individuals and associations advocating such reforms would have had beneficent effects at all comparable to those secured from the enactments of Parliament ? And yet Britain is famous for sturdy individualism, and her political life was long profoundly influenced by the Manchester School. Moreover, popular opinion in favour of social legislation in the United Kingdom has been given a driving force by the enfranchisement of the people which would otherwise have been lacking. Beneficent social legislation was scarcely attempted before the passing of the Reform Act in 1832.

The modern State, when based on democratic ideals, is not an external body to which its inhabitants go pleading for assistance and amelioration. It is, and ought to be, the concentrated and directing instrument of society as a whole. It is because we are convinced that the evils of India have gone far beyond the limits of successful remedy by merely sectional or individual efforts—though these are essential allies of progress—that we need the whole energy of the country as represented by the State, to pursue those radical reforms which can only come when the powers of society are behind them. A firm conviction that India is too large and too widespread, with too many natural divisions of climate and race, to take up the direct work of national regeneration so long overdue, leads to the conclusion that only province states with reasonable limits of area and population, and yet not too small to provide the resources required and develop strong local patriotism, will raise the peoples of the great peninsula to their legitimate standing in the world.

We have taken the most successful nationalities of Europe as providing approximate models in size and population for our province states. We have also suggested that the historical and natural causes that go to individualise each province should be taken into account for marking its limits and character. And within the provinces we advocate as wide a basis as possible of representation, because we are convinced that national regeneration is impossible if only the more favoured strata of society put their backs to the wheel. The ordinary franchise adopted in Europe would not bring forward in India the classes and castes that have long remained behind in the race of life. Since I am not proposing for the India of to-day some ideal system for a distant future I maintain that communal representation should be accepted throughout. It must not be forgotten that the various races and religions of India each have a more or less complex social system of their own to which they attach great importance, that such matters as marriage and divorce, the rites and ceremonies of family or communal life, are settled and arranged by the communal leaders on the basis of the sacred writings, traditions, and sometimes the environment of their peoples. This communal bond varies, no doubt, in degree; frequently it is highly organised and powerful, but sometimes at the other end of the scale it is only held together like sand. Still, in all cases, it has a part to play in the life of the nation, and if the autonomy to be built up in India is to be a natural evolution it must take account of the internal and sectional governing methods which the congeries of India have historically developed.

If a communal basis is set aside, the only way left of meeting the needs of India would be that of proportional representation with manhood suffrage. No system of proportional representation fair to all can be invented without universal suffrage. Without this safeguard the system degenerates into a form of class hegemony. In India, where its principles would be liable to much misunderstanding by the ill-educated, it would inevitably tend to perpetuate an unnatural state of society and to keep the backward communities where they are. Can any political thinker regard as possible for India universal suffrage, plus proportional representation, seeing that this would mean in many cases swollen constituencies returning fifteen or perhaps a score of members? Nor would manhood suffrage, assuming its possibility, give to each large community any such sense of national responsibility as will be derived from the fact that its members will be directly called upon, as such, to share in the political fabric.

Let me speak, finally, of my conviction that a progressive, satisfied, and happy India would be the strongest pillar, next to the United Kingdom, of the British Empire. Strong winds with world forces driving them are moving Asia towards some great destiny. Germany and Turkey, Japan or China, dismembered Russia, the erstwhile Central Asian States—what influences will the play of world forces give to each for good or evil? While no man can answer these questions, Britain must remember that for more than 150 years she has been the first Power of Asia, and that the position of her vigorous daughter partners, Australia, New Zealand, and South Africa, would become dangerously weak if the great base of her Eastern authority, triangular India, were ever to fall into other hands. In India she has a natural foster-daughter that has imbibed her culture and liberalising ideals. What is to be the position of this adopted, fast-growing child in the scattered family of the foster-mother? I am convinced that England and India will answer this question in a way worthy of their respective history, traditions, poetry, and art. A solid yet unchafing union, based on esteem and mutual interest, on the memory of common sacrifice for imperishable principles and the cause of liberty, will unite the foster-child with the grown-up daughters of the aged and geographically small, but powerful and noble mother country into a great instrument for the good of mankind, working everywhere in co-operation from Ottawa to Calcutta, from London to Delhi, from Melbourne to Bombay, for one beneficent Empire under a beloved sovereign.

INDEX